LATIMER STUDIES 72

CW01021695

TO PLOUGH OR TO PREACH

MISSION STRATEGIES IN NEW ZEALAND DURING THE 1820s

BY MALCOLM FALLOON

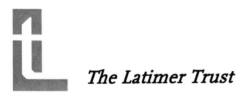

The Latimer Trust

To Plough or to Preach: Mission Strategies in New Zealand during the 1820s © Malcolm Falloon 2010

ISBN 978-0-946307-73-9

Cover photo: Marsden's Cross, Bay of Islands © John Winsley

Published by the Latimer Trust January 2010

The Latimer Trust (formerly Latimer House, Oxford) is a conservative Evangelical research organisation within the Church of England, whose main aim is to promote the history and theology of Anglicanism as understood by those in the Reformed tradition. Interested readers are welcome to consult its website for further details of its many activities.

The Latimer Trust
PO Box 26685, London N14 4XQ UK
Registered Charity: 1084337
Company Number: 4104465
Web: www.latimertrust.org
E-mail: administrator@latimertrust.org

Views expressed in works published by The Latimer Trust are those of the authors and do not necessarily represent the official position of The Latimer Trust.

Samuel Marsden's first service in New Zealand. The Gospel of Jesus Christ first proclaimed on these shores by the Rev. Samuel Marsden at Oihi, Bay of Islands, Christmas Day, 1814 [Christchurch] N.Z. Church Missionary Society [1964]. Painting by Russell Stuart Cedric Clark, 1905-1966, reproduced here by permission of the Alexander Turnbull Library, Wellington, New Zealand (Collection No. B-077-006).

This Study was submitted as a Research Essay to the University of Otago, New Zealand in November 2009. The author received a grant from The Latimer Trust which facilitated access to archive material, and this Study and the map below of the Bay of Islands, dating from c.1828, are published with the permission of the University of Otago.

Contents

1. Samuel Marsden.....................................4

2. The Wider Mission Debate.........................11

3. Marsden's Strategy 16

4. The Strategy Run Aground........................22

5. Henry Williams Arrives in New Zealand.....26

6. The State of the Mission............................28

7. Finding a New Way Forward......................30

8. Events Come to a Head 34

9. William's Critique of Marsden's Strategy....37

10. New Emphasis Proposed..........................41

11. Williams' Strategy Implemented 44

12. Marsden's Response................................53

13. Conclusion..56

14. Appendix..63

BIBLIOGRAPHY 70

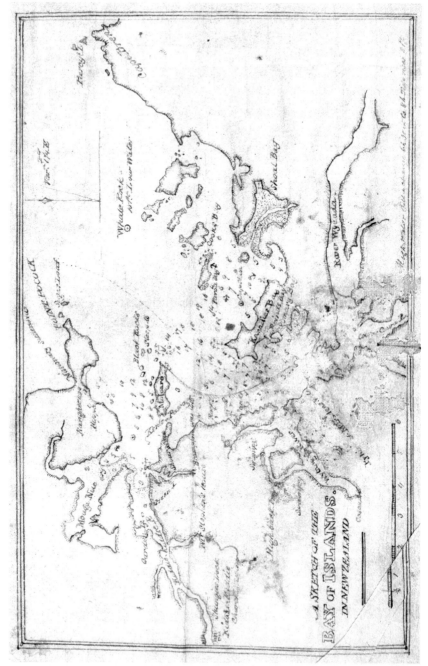

HM841.815 *Sketch of the Bay of Islands in New Zealand, c. 1828 (Hocken Collections, Uare Taoka o Hakena, University of Otago, PO Box 56, Dunedin, New Zealand).*

Introduction

One of the most significant events in the early history of New Zealand, must undoubtedly be the great turning of Maori to embrace the message of Christianity, Te Rongopai, in the 1830s. George Clarke, a former Bay of Islands missionary who became Protector of the Aborigines in the newly formed colonial government, estimated in 1845 that out of a population of 110,000 Maori, 64,000 were regularly attending the Anglican, Methodist or Roman Catholic mission services.[1] The figure is particularly startling, as Wright comments: "Only ten years before, in 1835, there had been but a handful of Maoris interested in Christianity. A few years before that there had been none. How did these remarkable changes come about?"[2] It has been a question much discussed by historians in recent years and a variety of contributing factors have been highlighted.[3]

The phenomena of such mass conversions to Christianity have been termed by missiologists as "People Movements,"[4] of which New Zealand was among the first of the modern missionary

---

[1] Harrison M. Wright, *New Zealand, 1769-1840: Early Years of Western Contact* (Cambridge, MA: Harvard University Press, 1959), 141.

[2] Ibid., 141.

[3] Wright, New Zealand, 1769-1840, 141-165; J.M.R. Owen, "Christianity and the Maoris to 1840," *New Zealand Journal of History* 2, no. 1 (1968): 18-40; Judith Binney, "Christianity and the Maoris to 1840: A Comment," *New Zealand Journal of History* 3, no. 2 (1969): 143-165; K.R. Howe, "The Maori Response to Christianity in the Thames-Waikato Area, 1833-1840," *New Zealand Journal of History* 7 (1973): 28-46; R. Fisher, "Henry Williams' Leadership of the CMS Mission to New Zealand," *New Zealand Journal of History* 9 (1975): 142-153; G Clover, "'Going Mihinare', 'Experimental Religion', and Maori Embracing of Missionary Christianity - A Re-Assessment," *Christian Brethren Research Fellowship Journal* 121, no. 1 (1990): 41-55; J.M.R. Owens, "New Zealand before Annexation," in *The Oxford History of New Zealand: Second Edition*, ed. Geoffrey W. Rice, 28-53 (Auckland: Oxford University Press, 1992).

[4] Alan R. Tippett, *People Movements in Southern Polynesia: Studies in the Dynamics of Church-planting and Growth in Tahiti, New Zealand, Tonga, and Samoa* (Chicago: Moody Press, 1971), 199. Clover, "Going Mihinare", 42.

movement – a movement that continues to reshape the face of world Christianity into the twenty first century.[5] In this regard, the events of the 1830's are not unique in world Christianity. Nor are New Zealand historians alone in expressing the work of the early missionaries in largely pejorative terms.[6] New Zealand historian Keith Sinclair's comment that the ideas of the missionaries are "as destructive as bullets" has set the tone for a number of subsequent writers.[7]

However, in a recent collection of essays, missions historian Dana Robert makes the comment that there has been a reassessment by historians of the paradigm of missionaries as "vehicles of 'cultural imperialism.'"[8] Instead the missionary should be treated as a "concrete actor in specific historical situations, and a participant in relationships with indigenous persons, who coexist in colonialist contexts and mutually influence each other."[9] She further maintains, along with her co-essayists, that the modern missionary movement should be treated as "neither idealism nor ideology, but as a pragmatic product of the historical encounter between Western Christianity and local settings."[10]

This essay seeks to explore two dominant mission strategies that shaped that encounter in the Church Missionary Society (CMS) mission to New Zealand during the 1820s. In particular, it will

---

[5] Waskom J. Pickett, *Christian Mass Movements in India: a Study with Recommendations,* 2nd Indian Edition (Lucknow, India: Lucknow, 1969), 36-56; Harold Turner, "New Religious Movements in Primal Societies," in *Australian Essays in World Religions,* 38-48 (Bedford Park, SA: The Australian Association for the Study of Religions, 1977), 38. Philip Jenkins, *The Next Christendom: the Coming of Global Christianity* (New York: Oxford University Press, 2002), 33-38.
[6] Jenkins, *The Next Christendom,* 39-42.
[7] Keith Sinclair, *A History of New Zealand,* revised ed. (Auckland: Penguin Books, 2000), 42; Judith Binney, *The Legacy of Guilt: A Life of Thomas Kendall,* (Wellington: Bridget Williams Books, 2005. First published by Oxford University Press, 1967), 23-46; Gavin McLean, *No Continuing City: A History of the Stone Store, Kerkeri* (Wellington: New Zealand Historic Places Trust, 1994), 11-30.
[8] Dana L. Robert, introduction to Robert, *Converting Colonialism,* 1.
[9] Ibid., 3.
[10] Ibid., 5.

explore the factors leading up to a change of direction for the mission in the year 1826, by drawing on correspondence between the two chief strategists, Samuel Marsden and Henry Williams, and their interaction with the CMS parent committee in London. Samuel Marsden, the supervisor of the mission, was based at Parramatta, New South Wales. He considered 'civilization' to be the herald of the Gospel; the necessary first step for Maori in receiving the Christian message and experiencing 'conversion'. However, Henry Williams, based at Paihia in the Bay of Islands, took a different view. He considered 'civilization' to be, not the herald, but the handmaiden of the Gospel. That 'conversion', rather than being a consequence of, was actually the prerequisite for the establishment of any lasting form of civilization. It was the tensions and synergies between these two views that helped shape the way the New Zealand mission was conducted during the 1820s. This in turn reflected the wider debate on mission strategy that was occurring during the early phase of the missionary movement.

1.   Samuel Marsden

In 1826 Samuel Marsden was 61 years old and was feeling the effects of age after many years of service as Chaplain to the Penal Colony of New South Wales. He had only recently come through a bruising encounter with the Colony's administration that also involved a brush with the Colonial Office in London.[11] Marsden wrote to Coates, the lay secretary of the CMS in September 1825, "I have never passed through more severe trials than what I have experienced from unreasonable and wicked men for the last three months."[12]

He first came to the Colony in 1794, cutting short his Cambridge University education, to take up the position of Assistant Chaplain, becoming the Senior Chaplain in the year 1800.[13] Marsden was from a rural Yorkshire background and did not begin his formal education until he was in his early twenties. He had received a scholarship from the Elland Society: a network of evangelical ministers who sponsored prospective ordination candidates from evangelical backgrounds without financial means. The Elland Society was founded in 1767 by Henry Venn, the vicar of Huddersfield, but met for most of its history, four times a year, in the nearby village of Elland.[14]

Being a "pensioner" of the Elland Society introduced Marsden to the inner circle of some of the most influential evangelicals within the Church of England, including William Wilberforce, the MP for Hull, an anti-slavery campaigner and philanthropist, who later

---

[11] A.T. Yarwood, *Samuel Marsden: The Great Survivor*, 2nd edition (Melbourne: Melbourne University Press, 1996), 245-250.
[12] Quoted in J. R. Elder, *The Letters and Journals of Samuel Marsden 1765-1838* (Dunedin: Wilkie & Reed for the Otago University Council, 1932), 55.
[13] Elder, *Letters and Journals*, 25-28.
[14] Ibid., 19.

supported Marsden in establishing the New Zealand mission. It was through Wilberforce's influence that Marsden had been offered the position of Assistant Chaplain to the Penal Colony.[15]

Marsden brought to the task of mission at least two important influences. Firstly, "there can be no doubt," as John Elder, the editor of his letters and journals says,

> "that it was his own training as artisan and farmer that made him lay such insistence upon the necessity in missionary enterprise of basing the structure of religious teaching upon a preliminary training in arts, crafts, and agriculture, and that caused him to demand that a missionary 'should also be naturally of an industrious turn; a man who could live in any country by dint of his own labour.'"[16]

However the second, and arguably the more important, influence was an evangelical humanitarianism that was part of the general outlook of the evangelical circles with which he was associated.[17] Both these influences shaped his thinking as he developed and deployed his mission strategy in the South Pacific.

Before he became involved in establishing the New Zealand mission, Marsden had become the agent for the London Missionary Society's mission in Tahiti and other Islands of Polynesia. The London Missionary Society (LMS) was a non-denominational mission organisation that predated the formation of the CMS by some four years. The LMS had decided upon Tahiti as the site for its first mission enterprise. In 1797 they sent out 29 missionaries in the *Duff* only to see most of them forced to abandon their stations in 1798 and be evacuated to Sydney. It is here that Marsden made his contact with the LMS, becoming their official agent in 1801 for the Tahitian

---

[15] Ibid., 20.
[16] Ibid., 18.
[17] Nigel A.D. Scotland, *Evangelical Anglicans in a Revolutionary Age: 1789-1901* (Carlisle: Paternoster, 2004), 27-49, 73-95.

mission.[18] It is probably here also, that Marsden observed the failure of the strategy that sought to first convert the hearer to the gospel before a measure of civilization had been attained.[19] This would explain why Marsden was keen to emphasise to the CMS in London that, "To preach the Gospel without the aid of the Arts will never succeed amongst the heathen for any time."[20] After many difficult years the mission met with remarkable success following the victory of King Pomare II over his enemies in 1815.[21]

Marsden, in commenting on the success of the mission, wrote these fighting words, which reflected his awareness of the wider debate concerning missionary methods occurring back in Britain:

> "Many, even sober-thinking men, for years viewed the Mission to the Islands with contempt; and considered it as the offspring of intemperate zeal. The mouths of gainsayers must now be stopped, and infidels silenced... Nothing like this, as I have had occasion before to remark, has occurred since the days of the Apostles... We must look beyond all second causes, to the Great First Cause; and, while we do this, we must use such means as are within our reach, and follow closely the openings of Providence."[22]

It was one of these "openings of Providence" that allowed Marsden to return to England in 1807 with the aim of persuading the CMS to establish a New Zealand mission. "There is," said Marsden, "a highly

---

[18] Elder, *Letters and Journals*, 41.

[19] Niel Gunson, *Messengers of Grace: Evangelical Missionaries in the South Seas, 1797-1860* (Melbourne: Oxford University Press, 1978), 270.

[20] Allan K. Davidson and Peter J. Lineham, *Transplanted Christianity: Documents illustrating aspects of New Zealand Church History*, 2nd edition (Palmerston North: Dunmore Press, 1989), 26-27.

[21] Tippett, *People Movements*, 9-26; Tom Hiney, *On the Missionary Trail: A Journey Through Polynesia, Asia, and Africa with the London Missionary Society* (New York: Grove Press, 2000), 61-62.

[22] *Missionary Register*, 1820, 127.

favourable dispensation of Providence towards myself at that time... to gratify my earnest desire of having the Gospel preached at New Zealand."[23]

The concept of God's providence was a constant theme in Marsden's writings and explains much of his resilience through very difficult times; that despite the set backs, in the end the Gospel would win through. For Marsden, even the disappointments and disasters were under God's control: "All things are wisely ordered for our good," he writes to Wilberforce, even if "there is not a single event in our lives for which we can assign all the reasons which Infinite Wisdom may have in view."[24]

Along with a belief in the "openings of Providence", and perhaps because of it, Marsden had a very practical, almost empirical, approach to mission strategy; his mission practice was developed from observation rather than from theory. This explains much of the reason why Marsden was at first reluctant to pursue a separate mission to the Australian Aborigines. Yarwood comments on Marsden's failure to establish an aboriginal mission: "The natives have no reflection – they have no attachments, and they have no wants. By rejecting the material civilisation of the European they baulked at what he [Marsden] saw as the necessary first step towards conversion."[25]

It was economic development, or commerce, that Marsden saw as the "first step" for Maori to rank with "civilized nations" and for them to enjoy the "blessings which Christianity imparts."[26] It was something he modelled in his own situation in New South Wales with his own interest in farming and trade. Marsden observed on his fourth visit to New Zealand in 1823 that,

---

[23] Quoted in Elder, *Letters and Journals*, 42.
[24] Quoted in Elder, *Letters and Journals*, 56.
[25] A.T. Yarwood, "Samuel Marsden," *Australian Dictionary of Evangelical Biography*, ed. Brian Dickey (Sydney: Evangelical History Assosciation, 1994), 250.
[26] Elder, *Letters and Journals*, 371.

"The introduction of tools of agriculture, such as axes, hoes, spades, has encouraged very extensive cultivation in every district, and it is extending more and more every day. To give a man a spade is not like giving him 100lb. of potatoes to supply his immediate wants, but it is furnishing him with the means of raising many hundreds. This is evident in every part of New Zealand."[27]

It is statements like these that revealed Marsden's humanitarian spirit, the same spirit that motivated so many English evangelicals to not only reform their own English society but to confront the global evils of the slave trade. Similar sentiments were later expressed by a friend and supporter of Marsden's, the anti-slavery campaigner Thomas Buxton, who maintained that the only way for the slave trade to be finally stopped in Africa was through economic development: "The real remedy, the true ransom for Africa, will be found in her fertile soil."[28]

It would be wrong, however, to see Marsden's attempt at bringing civilisation to Maori as a simplistic endeavour to replicate a refined English society in the South Pacific. His understanding was far grander than that entirely. He wanted to create a self-sustaining Christian nation, fully integrated by trade links into a global economy. It was something that Marsden took every opportunity to encourage. An example of this occurred during his 1823 visit to New Zealand, when several chiefs visited him on board the *Brampton* and conversation turned to why it was that the missionaries did not sell muskets and powder. Taua, the son of Te Pahi and who had also stayed with Marsden in Parramatta, made the observation:

"We are, at present, in the same state as the Otaheitans [Tahitians] were some time back. The Otaheitans wanted only muskets and powder, and would have nothing else; and now,

---

[27] Ibid., 371.
[28] Andrew F. Walls, "The Legacy of Thomas Foxwell Buxton," *International Bulletin of Missionary Research* 15, no. 2 (April 1991): 74-78.

as they know better, they want none. The New Zealanders will care nothing about them, when they know better; which they will in time, but time must be allowed them to learn better."[29]

Marsden then seized the opportunity to make a point about trade, for only the day before a brig owned by King Pomare of Tahiti, the *Queen Charlotte*, had sailed from the Bay:

> "the Otaheitans had sent oil and various other articles to Port Jackson, for which they had received, in return, tea, sugar, flour, and such clothing as they wanted; and that the New Zealanders might, in time, have a ship of their own to procure sperm-oil, spars, etc., which they could sell at Port Jackson; and that many of them were able to kill whales, having been employed on board the Whalers. When they got a vessel of their own, they would soon be equal to the Otaheitans, and give over their cruel wars. They expressed much pleasure in the idea of having a vessel of their own, to enable them to procure what they want."[30]

In Marsden's mind there was a strong link between agriculture and civilisation, a product not only of his love of farming, but also his love for the Old Testament: "I anticipate the day, when he will plough with his yoke of oxen, like the ancient Prophets; and rejoice with the joy of harvest, when his crops are gathered in."[31] In expressing his disapproval of muskets and gunpowder to the missionary settlers in 1819, Marsden advocated agriculture as the only way that such an evil could be restrained:

> "Saws, spades, hoes, and axes will civilize them, and induce domestic and commercial habits; will give them something to eat and to sell, and will prepare them for receiving the Gospel. The Settlers may plough and preach: they will then make a

---

[29] Elder, *Letters and Journals*, 352.
[30] Ibid., 353.
[31] *Missionary Register*, 1820, 307.

happy nation of them."[32]

Marsden's strategy of to "plough and preach" was so that Maori might become both civilised and Christianized. It was the same emphasis that was later expressed by missionary strategists such as Buxton, Venn and Livingstone.[33] So, for instance, Marsden would have heartily supported Buxton's plea for the African Mission:

> "Let missionaries and schoolmasters, the plough and the spade, go together, and agriculture will flourish; the avenues to legitimate commerce will be opened; confidence between man and man will be inspired; whilst civilization will advance as the natural effect, and Christianity operate as the proximate cause of this happy change."[34]

If the reality of Marsden's assessment of Maori was one of inferiority, his vision for the future paid them the highest of compliments; he saw no reason why Maori could not take their place in the world on an equal footing with any other civilised nation.[35]

---

[32] Ibid., 1820, 307.
[33] Andrew F. Walls, "The Legacy of David Livingstone," *International Bulletin of Missionary Research* 11, no. 3 (July 1987): 125-129.
[34] Walls, "Thomas Buxton," 74-78.
[35] Missionary Register, 1820, 306.

2.   The Wider Mission Debate

As previously mentioned, Marsden's ideas concerning mission strategy were influenced by his observations of the failed LMS mission to Tahiti in 1797 – 1801. The London Missionary Society (or just the Missionary Society as it was called in its early days) was itself the product of a remarkable upsurge of interest in world mission. This had begun to take place as Marsden was departing England to take up the chaplaincy at Port Jackson. Congregational and evangelical Christians alike were united by a common conviction that God had called them to the grand task of world evangelism. It was this new and radical ecumenical spirit, that led to the founding of the LMS in 1795 along non-denominational lines.[36] Of the 25 Directors of the LMS, perhaps the three most influential figures were John Eyre, David Bogue and Thomas Haweis.[37]

Of the three, Haweis and Bogue were particularly influential in framing the mission policies of the LMS, yet both men had significant areas of disagreement as to how the mission should be conducted. It was Haweis who had advocated the establishment of the Tahiti Mission. He had made a systematic study of the world and had come to the conclusion that the South Pacific was the most suitable place to begin.

> "Peculiarly favourable circumstances will engage attention to these countries. The fertility of the soil – the beauty and healthiness of the climate – the uncivilised state of the natives, which gives Europeans so great an advantage over them – the facility wherewith settlements may be formed –

---

[36]   Stuart Piggin, *Making Evangelical Missionaries 1789-1858: The Social Background, Motives and Training of British Prostestant Missionaries to India* (Courtenay Press, 1984) 107-110.

[37] Arthur Skevington Wood, *Thomas Haweis: 1734-1820* (London: SPCK, 1957), 194.

and the easiness with which they can be maintained – besides the probability, that the spirit of commerce and adventure will make some essay to secure the first advantages, and forward civilisation, if the gospel which we have sent them should not by its own divine power produce all the happy effects upon the natives, which we hope and expect to hear."[38]

Bogue, however, was unpersuaded and favoured instead missionaries being sent to the British colony in India, even offering to go himself as a missionary to Bengal:

> "The plan of sending out young men unaccustomed to the task of religious instruction never appeared to me calculated to produce the end we had in view. I always thought it the duty of more experienced men to lead the way, and offer themselves for the service of the heathen."[39]

Both men did agree that the success of any mission depended ultimately on the preaching of the Gospel of Christ. Haweis, from his personal experience of the evangelical revival at Truro, knew the impact that the plain preaching of the Gospel could have (at least in England):

> "Brethren, our whole success will depend upon this one point: if Christ be preached, only preached, always preached, then we shall see the power of His death and resurrection, and the Lord will add again 'daily to His church such as shall be saved.'"[40]

Where the two disagreed, was in selecting the type of missionary to do the preaching. What Haweis believed to be required was,

> "A plain man, with a good natural understanding, well read in

---

[38] Thomas Haweis, *An Impartial and Succinct History of the Rise, Declension, and Revival of the Church of Christ*, vol. 3 (London, 1800), 335.

[39] James Bennett, *Memoirs of the Life of Rev. David Bogue, D.D.* (London, 1827), 205; Piggin, *Making Evangelical Missionaries*, 156,168.

[40] Skevington Wood, *Thomas Haweis*, 198.

the Bible, full of faith and the Holy Ghost, though he comes from the forge, or the shop, would, I own, in my view, as a missionary to the heathen, be infinitely preferable to all the learning of the schools, and would possess, in the skill and labour of his hands, advantages which barren science could never compensate."[41]

Bogue, however, took a different view. In the words of James Bennett, his early biographer:

"There have not ceased to be men of influence in the society [LMS], who sincerely think that the best education for missionaries is none at all; and the next best is that which consists in teaching them to make wheelbarrows and plant turnips, rendering them useful mechanics and agriculturists rather than good divines or preachers. David Bogue, however, was deeply convinced that Christ, instead of sending his apostles to learn to catch fish, called them away from ships and nets, to follow him, and learn to become fishers of men."[42]

Behind these differences probably lay a number of cultural and personal factors. Haweis did not come from a well-to-do family and could not afford to go to university until an evangelical vicar at Oxford, Joseph Jane, convinced him to enrol and covered all his expenses. Bogue, on the other hand was a Presbyterian from Scotland and carried with him that strong Scottish emphasis on education. In Bogue's view, the missionary required:

"two distinguishing qualities in an eminent degree – knowledge and zeal. His knowledge of divine things should exceed those of an ordinary pastor of a church already formed; because from him a whole country may receive its views of the Gospel, and be cast as it were into his mould. And how

---

[41] Ibid., 198.
[42] Bennett, *Memoirs,* 220.

pure and full should his ideas of the gospel be!"[43]

The reason why Bogue urged a higher level of education for missionaries was because he also believed that it was their chief task to raise up and train indigenous missionaries and clergy to carry on the work of evangelism.[44]

In this debate between the two leaders it becomes clear that Haweis proposed a model whereby the missionary would work to at least "secure the first advantages" of civilization of which Christianity was the capstone. The labours of the missionary would be aided by the divine power that comes through the preaching of the Gospel, to bring about the necessary transformation. Christianity and 'civilisation' were on the same continuum, though not confused with one another. Under this model, a person might be civilized and yet still not a Christian, but there could not be such a thing as an uncivilized Christian!

> "The amelioration of the condition of the wretched peasantry, must advance with habits of industry and the profits of manufactures and agriculture. Ignorance and superstition will receive some check from the introduction of more enlightened intelligence; and, may we not hope the more happy diffusion of gospel truth which hath already begun, will increase abundantly."[45]

David Bogue believed that missionaries should have nothing to do with the work of civilizing people. Again James Bennett, Bogue's biographer, speaks for him when he said, "missionaries are not fitted for the task; and if they were, it is not their proper business."[46] David Bogue viewed the civilized countries of the world as the most suitable for Christian mission, for they were the most 'rational' and would therefore capitulate more easily to the Christian religion. Under this

---

[43] Ibid., 188.
[44] Piggin, *Making Evangelical Missionaries*, 178-179.
[45] Thomas Haweis, *The Blessings of Peace* (London, 1801), 12.
[46] Bennett, *Memoirs*, 220-221.

model, civilization is essentially equated with rationality and hence Bogue's emphasis on education.[47] This would place Bogue in the slightly unusual position of advocating a rational Calvinist system of thought rather than an expected evangelical perspective. The rational Calvinist theory viewed the "rise of Christianity as a necessary historical moment to be repeated in every civilized society, given the correct conditions."[48]

Marsden had a very similar background to that of Haweis; both were from the lower-middle class and both had been sponsored into the Anglican ministry by evangelical leaders. So it is understandable that Marsden's sympathies should lie with Haweis rather than with Bogue. Haweis' confidence in the ability of "a plain man...full of faith" would have made sense to Marsden. But Marsden would have questioned his over-confidence in the plain preaching of the Gospel to alone bring about the changes that were sought. This did not match with Marsden's observations of the matter. He saw the need for civilization to precede the reception of the gospel, or at least for them to go hand in hand with one another. This might indicate an influence of Bogue and the Scottish Enlightenment[49], though Marsden saw the civilizing influence to be the 'Arts' rather than 'reason'. It may also have simply been the received wisdom of the Christian public of his day.

---

[47] Piggin, *Making of Evangelical Missionaries*, 180.

[48] Ian Douglas Maxwell, "Civilization or Christianity? The Scottish Debate on Mission Methods, 1750-1835," in Stanley, *Christian Missions and the Enlightenment*, 130-131.

[49] See the discussion in Brian Stanley, "Christianity and Civilization in English Evangelical Mission Thought, 1792-1857," in Stanley *Christian Missions and the Enlightenment*, 187.

3.   Marsden's Strategy

Marsden had travelled to England to gain permission from CMS to recruit missionaries for the New Zealand Mission. This was not an easy task, as, since its formation, the CMS had had great difficulty in attracting suitable candidates, especially clergy. In the light of this problem, the CMS Secretary of the day, John Venn, had said, "I would rather send out Laymen than none at all; and allow Laymen to perform many functions usually confined to Ministers at home."[50] This fitted well with Marsden's convictions:

> "Since nothing, in my opinion, can pave the way for the introduction of the Gospel, but civilization; and that can only be accomplished amongst the heathen by the arts; I would recommend that Three Mechanics be appointed to make the first attempt."[51]

In one sense, Marsden's scheme turned a necessity into a virtue for the CMS and allowed them to harness the full strength of the evangelical movement in England to the missionary cause. In any case, an official plan to preach the Gospel using laymen would have laid the CMS open to charges of 'Methodism'! The leadership of the Established Church and the general culture viewed spiritual matters as very much the preserve of the clergy. Marsden's early biographer, J. B. Marsden (who is not related), reports that the CMS in 1815 felt it necessary to distance itself from Marsden's view:

> "It has been stated that the mission was originally established, and for a long time systematically conducted, on the principle of first civilizing and then Christianizing the natives. This is wholly a mistake. The agents employed in establishing the

---

[50] Davidson and Lineham, *Transplanted Christianity*, 25.
[51] Davidson & Lineham, *Transplanted Christianity*, 26.

mission were laymen, because clergymen could not be had; and the instructions given to them necessarily correspond with their lay character."[52]

It is unclear whether this reference has been dated correctly by J.B. Marsden or whether the 'mission' referred to was the CMS mission in general, as no source is given. If the latter, then the comment is not made with New Zealand specifically in mind. Either way, it would be hard to say that in 1815 the New Zealand mission had been "for a long time systematically conducted," for it had only just begun. But it does indicate that there was no firm policy from the Parent Committee in support of Samuel Marsden's strategy, and that some, at least, supported him for pragmatic reasons only.

However, Marsden succeeded in getting the backing of the CMS for a New Zealand mission. As a result of his trip to England, he had recruited William Hall (a carpenter), John King (a shoemaker and twine spinner) and Thomas Kendall (a school teacher and farmer), along with their families and a number of assistants; 25 persons in all. They arrived in the Bay of Islands aboard the *Active* that Marsden had newly purchased for the use of the mission. The first mission station was established in December 1814 at Rangihoua, under the protection of the local chief, Ruatara.[53] Marsden's plan was that by their industry ("arts") and family life the missionaries were to gain the attention of Maori so that the Christian message might be communicated. "I do not mean," said Marsden in outlining his scheme to the CMS,

> "that a native should learn to build a hut or make an axe before he should be told any thing of Man's Fall and Redemption; but that these grand subjects should be introduced at every favourable opportunity, while the natives

[52] J. B. Marsden, *Life and Work of Samuel Marsden* (Christchurch, 1913), 42.
[53] A.T. Yarwood, *Samuel Marsden*, 174-180; Patricia Bawden, *The Years Before Waitangi: A Story of Early Maori/European Contact in New Zealand* (Auckland: Benton Ross, 1987), 76-83.

are learning any of their simple arts. To preach the Gospel without the aid of the Arts will never succeed amongst the heathen for any time."[54]

This clarification of his strategy allows us to see the interaction of his confidence in God's providence ('every favourable opportunity') with his empirical approach to mission, based on his experience with the LMS mission to Tahiti. However, Marsden did seem to go further when he suggested that civilisation and conversion were linked in some manner, although he did not confuse or conflate the two:

> "commerce and the arts having a natural tendency to inculcate industrious and moral habits, open a way for the introduction of the Gospel, and lay the foundation for its continuance when once received."[55]

Four years later, on his second visit to New Zealand in 1819, Marsden was still convinced of the link between civilization and Christianity. But he also added additional support from a humanitarian appeal to the Bible:

> "Their temporal situation must be improved by agriculture and the simple arts in order to lay a permanent foundation for the introduction of Christianity. It may be reasonably expected that their moral and religious advancement will keep pace with the increase of their temporal comforts. They are at present naked and hungry, and if we should say unto them: 'Be ye warmed and filled' notwithstanding we give them not those things that be needful for the body, what doth it profit? I am sure the bowels of the Christian World would yearn over their temporal and spiritual miseries was it possible to make them known."[56]

Again, it was comments like these, inserted into journals for public

---

[54] Davidson & Lineham, *Transplanted Christianity*, 26-27.
[55] Marsden, *Life and Work*, 40.
[56] Elder, *Letters and Journals*, 167. The biblical quote is from James 2:15-16.

circulation, that indicated Marsden's awareness of his critics with regard to the strategy adopted for the Australasian missions.

As well as mission stations based in New Zealand, Marsden's strategy also involved the setting up of a "seminary" for young Maori leaders at Parramatta (New South Wales, Australia) where he lived. This had developed informally at first, from the hospitality that Marsden had extended to visiting Maori. But it took on a more formal nature in 1815 after the New Zealand Mission had commenced.[57] Marsden had returned to New South Wales from the Bay of Islands with ten Maori, eight of whom were the sons of chiefs.[58] The intention was for them to learn simple agricultural skills and be exposed to the worship and beliefs of the Christian faith. For instance, if they learnt how to use a bullock team, Marsden generously suggested that they would be allowed to take it home with them when they returned.[59]

The Seminary also eased Marsden's concerns for the safety of the Settlers, for it gave him a number of "hostages" with him in Parramatta.[60] Safety was something that he felt had been sadly neglected by the first LMS mission, which had caused him to recommend to their Directors that missionaries should be allowed some form of 'self-defence'.[61] But the effects of the trade in muskets and powder on Polynesia convinced him that personal friendship, Maori hospitality and mutual self-interest should be all that the New Zealand Mission should rely upon. Safety concerns were what led Marsden, in the early years of the mission, to oppose those who wanted to move their base away from the relative safety of Rangihoua, across the bay to Waitangi.[62]

The greater aim of the Seminary, however, was to train up a

---

[57] Elder, *Letters and Journals*, 39.
[58] Yarwood, *Samuel Marsden*, 180.
[59] *Missionary Register*, 1820, 304-305.
[60] Elder, *Letters and Journals*, 39.
[61] Marsden, *Life and Work*, 26-27.
[62] Marsden to the Secretary, 3 March 1817, in Elder, *Letters and Journals*, 224-225.

group of young leaders who would form the nucleus of a band of indigenous evangelists upon their return to New Zealand.[63] The work of the Seminary was a practical laboratory for Marsden's mission theory, allowing the seminarians opportunity to be exposed to 'civilization' and looking for them, "God willing," to embrace the Christian faith. Certainly, Marsden was pleased with the initial impressions: "They see such a difference between our civilized and their savage state, that they cannot be persuaded that the same God made both them and us."[64]

In addition to Maori staying at Parramatta, it should also be noted that a number of Polynesians from the LMS missions were in residence and were able to interact with Maori alongside Europeans.[65] From these contacts, Maori learnt of the influence of Christianity in Tahiti; as in the previously noted example of Taua, the son Te Pahi, who was resident in Parramatta for more than 12 months.[66] There was also direct contact between the Islands of Polynesia and New Zealand. Kendall reported that a group of Tahitian sailors had visited the Bay of Islands in 1819:

> "On the Sunday after Easter, I had an opportunity to examine some Otaheitean Sailors, belonging to the Ship King George. They read the works of their Missionaries, both in print and manuscript, very readily. It would have rejoiced your heart to have been with us on that day. The New Zealanders fell on their knees, and continued to behave with decency and listen with attention, while they heard prayer in their own tongue, and while the Otaheitean sailors in the evening were reading in my house and singing the praises of their Redeemer. These Christian Islanders would not take a mouthful of victuals until they had implored the Divine Blessing; nor would they

---

[63] *Missionary Register*, 1820, 305.
[64] Marsden to the Secretary, 24 February 1819; *Missionary Register*, 1820, 304. Elder, *Letters and Journals*, 231.
[65] *Missionary Register*, 1826, 157.
[66] Elder, *Letters and Journals*, 352.

leave the table until they had given thanks. They slept in one of our barns, and spent part of the night in singing and prayer."[67]

The effect of the Tahitian sailors on local Maori was all the more dramatic when contrasted with the usual behaviour of sailors who entered The Bay and the largely ineffective work of the missionaries up to that point in time.

---

[67] *Missionary Register*, 1820, 308.

4. The Strategy Run Aground

Although Marsden had reported rather optimistically after his second visit to New Zealand in 1819 that "important preparatory progress has been made,"[68] things were not going well. The chief trouble, which started almost immediately, was internal conflicts between the settlers. At first, Marsden put this down to issues of personal character and the unsuitability of particular individuals for the rigours of the missionary environment.[69]

But increasingly, Marsden saw that the root of the problem was the practise of 'private trading', where each missionary looked to barter with local Maori for their own advantage instead of the mutual benefit for the mission as a whole.[70] There were several attempts to form an agreement together to cease the practice but they were soon broken and the trading continued. Eventually, the main items of private trade became, much to Marsden's horror, muskets and powder! The argument from the missionaries was that they were forced to pursue the trade out of necessity, in order to obtain the supplies they desperately needed. Marsden would not accept such an excuse, as he believed the threat of withdrawing the missionaries back to New South Wales (and carrying out the threat if necessary) would have quickly levelled the playing field in that regard.[71] The problems came when the members of the mission were divided and some continued to trade at the expense of the others.

"All the difficulties in New Zealand that I have met with have been in governing the Europeans. They will not do what is

---

[68] *Missionary Register,* 1822,93.
[69] Marsden to Hall and King, 7 December, 1816, in Elder, *Letters and Journals,* 223; Marsden to the Secretary, 3 March 1817, Elder, *Letters and Journals,* 224-226.
[70] Marsden to the Settlers, 24 February, 1819, in Elder, *Letters and Journals,* 232-233.
[71] Marsden to Kendall, 26 April, 1820, in Elder, *Letters and Journals,* 333.

right. They will not live in unity and brotherly love. The love of money, the thirst for pre-eminence, the want of industry and zeal for the good of the heathen, have greatly mitigated against the success of the Mission. I had used every persuasion and every means in my power to put a stop to the abominable traffic in muskets and powder. I had obtained their solemn pledges, signed with their own signatures, that they would put away this accursed thing. I relied upon their promises. Before I left New Zealand I found these promises broken. The promises were renewed, but on my return in February I then found myself deceived again and that no confidence was to be placed in them."[72]

So, for Marsden, the problems in New Zealand were not so much due to the overall strategy itself, but with its ineffective delivery. "When I reflect," said Marsden in 1823, "upon the evils which have crept in among the missionaries, I am astonished that the Mission has not been completely annihilated."[73] Marsden's only consolation was that similar problems had occurred in the LMS mission in Tahiti and such things, regrettably, were only to be expected:

> "Had I not persevered in urging the missionaries of the London Missionary Society from time to time to return to their work in the Society Islands, when they came despairing and had given up the cause altogether and told me it was no use, the heathen in theses islands would not now have cast their gods, their idols, into the fire.[74]

However, the missionaries themselves became aware that, quite apart from the internal disputes, there were more fundamental problems involved in implementing the strategy. Maori were by no means convinced that they needed the civilizing arts that the missionaries were attempting to impart. For example, William Hall wrote

---

[72] Marsden to the Secretary, 22 September 1820, in Elder, *Letters and Journals,* 331.
[73] *Missionary Register,* 1824, 516.
[74] Marsden to the Secretary, 3 March 1817, in Elder, *Letters and Journals,* 225-226.

despairingly in 1816,

> "I find it is almost impracticable to make Mechanics of them or to teach them the Arts at New Zealand. They are not arrived at that state yet, I cannot work amongst them, they pilfer the Tools so much, they have at different times stolen my working axes so that I have not had one left to do any thing with... I have used my utmost exertion since I came to New Zealand, in striving to establish an eligible settlement as a means of supporting ourselves, but I find my designs all obstructed, and I have almost paid too dear for making the experiment."[75]

There were other setbacks as well, such as the costs of maintaining the *Active* in service (which eventually had to be sold)[76] and the deaths from disease of seven young Maori living at Parramatta.

> "These young persons belonged to the first families in the Bay of Islands. How mysterious are the ways of God! They are past finding out. I had fondly imagined that some of these Youths who are now no more, would, upon their return to their native country, have promoted the general welfare of their countrymen; and have forwarded, by their superior knowledge of civil life, their civilisation. But God's ways are not as our ways, neither are His thoughts as our thoughts."[77]

The most devastating blow came when Hongi Hika returned from his trip to England with Kendall, ready to go to war with his newly purchased muskets.[78] Of all people, Hongi was best placed to benefit from the civilizing effects of the missionaries, yet he was the one most bent on war with his southern neighbours. The missionaries had noted his change in demeanour towards them and an increased

---

[75] Davidson & Lineham, *Transplanted Christianity*, 29-30.
[76] Marsden to the Secretary, 3 March 1817, in Elder, *Letters and Journals*, 224-225; Marsden to the Secretary, 7 February 1820, in Elder, *Letters and Journals*, 328-329.
[77] *Missionary Register*, 1822, 393.
[78] Elder, *Letters and Journals*, 342.

resistance by Maori in The Bay to both their temporal and spiritual endeavours.[79] Such was the state of the mission when Henry Williams arrived in New Zealand in August 1823.

---

[79] *Missionary Register*, 1823, 67-68 & 506.

5.   Henry Williams Arrives in New Zealand

Henry Williams was a former officer in the Royal Navy before becoming a missionary with CMS, and had been involved in a number of naval engagements during the Napoleonic wars. Williams' biographer comments that his interest in coming to New Zealand was sparked by the thought of it being the most difficult and dangerous of the missions then operated by the CMS.[80]

Before applying to CMS, he had married Marianne Coldham, who "entered the marriage with full knowledge and, indeed, anticipation of the hazardous future planned."[81] In reply to their farewell "charge" from the CMS Committee, Williams declared, "With regard to Mrs Williams, I beg to say she does not accompany me merely as my wife, but as a fellow helper in the work."[82] While waiting to be deployed, he also took the opportunity to train in surgery, medicine and boat building.[83]

Williams had been warned concerning the state of the New Zealand Mission,[84] and the reality of arriving in the Bay of Islands could surely not have left him disappointed. There were two existing Mission Stations by this stage, Rangihoua and Kerikeri, with two missionary families at each. Marsden's intention was that Williams should establish a third at Paihia to honour a promise he made to the local chief, Te Koki, and his wife, whose son had died while staying at Parramatta. The Williams family settled at Paihia along with William

---

[80] Lawrence M. Rogers, *Te Wiremu: A Biography of Henry Williams* (Christchurch: Pegasus, 1973), 34-35. Hugh Carleton, *The Life of Henry Williams* (Auckland, 1874), 15.
[81] Rogers, *Te Wiremu*, 37.
[82] Hugh Carleton, *The Life of Henry Williams*, 19.
[83] Ibid., 16; Rogers, *Te Wiremu*, 36.
[84] By his mentor and confidante, the Revd E.G. Marsh. Rogers, *Te Wiremu*, 36-37.

Fairburn, a carpenter, and his family. Paihia had the decided advantage of being further away from the assembly point for Maori war parties at Kerikeri and the more dubious one of being closer to the shipping that would anchor across the bay at Kororareka (Russell).

6.   The State of the Mission

Just how hazardous it was to live in their new home must have been reinforced when the *Brampton*, the ship returning Marsden and John Butler and his family to "the Colony" (New South Wales), was wrecked as it began its voyage; fortunately everyone managed to scramble to safety.[85] However, there were deeper troubles in evidence, not the least of which was the fall-out from the actions of Thomas Kendall and John Butler. Kendall, who was the leader of the first band of "settlers" to come to New Zealand in 1814, had been dismissed the previous year for adultery, but continued to live in the area. Butler, who had replaced Kendall as leader, had just been removed by Marsden. In fact, one of Williams' first duties was to chair the board of inquiry investigating the allegation of drunkenness against him;[86] though there seems to have been more to the dismissal than just that charge.[87]

The difficulties over leadership had been brewing for sometime and had left the missionary community demoralised and rife with quarrels and no doubt deeply suspicious of the leadership that Williams would supply. Williams reported in those first few months, that his chairing of the monthly meeting of missionaries "requires the utmost care" as there was still an "inflammatory air hovering about."[88]

However, external threats to the mission were helping to bind the new team together. One of these threats was the presence of Kendall, who was still in The Bay and maintained his friendship with

[85] Elder, *Letters and Journals*, 339.
[86] Special Meeting, 6 November 1823, *CMS Archives*, CNM3, 88; Elder, *Letters and Journals*, 398.
[87] Elder, *Letters and Journals*, 401-402.
[88] H Williams to the Secretaries, 21 November 1823, *CMS Archives*, CNM3, 87.

Hongi Hika. Hongi was determined that Kendall should have his old house back at Kerikeri. Williams and Kemp stood their ground and told Hongi that he and Kendall would have to enter by force. It was not the reply that Hongi or Kendall had expected. In this test of wills, Williams had brought a new strength to the missionaries' resolve. While they awaited Hongi's next move, Williams comments that they were bound together in prayer.[89]

---

[89] Ibid., 80-81.

7.   Finding a New Way Forward

In Williams' assessment of the mission, the highest priority had to be placed on obtaining their own boat.[90] It was not only prudent for the well-being of the mission, but was essential if Williams was to implement his emerging ideas for the mission. With that in mind, he commenced building a vessel in July 1824 thinking that it would take him three months. In fact it wasn't until nineteen months later in January 1826 that the boat was completed. The building of a boat was something that he had already discussed with Marsden who was in agreement and prepared to invest £250 of his own money into the project.

Marsden had in mind a modest vessel that could ply the waters of The Bay and perhaps in the Summer months explore further down the coast, but Williams had "more extensive nautical ideas."[91] Williams' strategy required a boat big enough to make the 5-10 day voyage to Port Jackson in New South Wales; this would give the mission greater freedom to source its food supplies from further afield and circumvent the musket trade that monopolized all the surplus food in The Bay.

From London, the building of the *Herald* (as the completed vessel was named) must have been viewed with increasing concern; was the New Zealand Mission being consumed by temporal matters?[92] Williams was at pains to justify his actions and to convince them of its value. The *Herald* was the key to alleviating the problem with food. But Williams also saw the strategic opportunity of taking things a step further and relieving the mission entirely of its need to

---

[90] H Williams to the Secretaries, 31 December 1824, *CMS Archives*, CNM3, 297.
[91] *Missionary Register*, 1824, 410.
[92] As evidenced by Williams' need to reassure the parent committee. H Williams to the Secretaries, 31 December 1824, *CMS Archives*, CNM3, 297.

supply its own food. By bringing in supplies, resources that were currently bound up in farming could be released and invested in language learning, schools and itinerant preaching.

To achieve those three objectives, there needed to be a greater degree of 'local control'. Marsden was unlikely to approve of them given his past policies. Part of that need for local control of the overall direction of the mission was a natural consequence of living in a remote part of the world, where long delays in communication were to be expected. For instance, Williams complained to London in September 1825 that he had not received a letter since he had arrived in New Zealand over two years ago. One can sympathize with Williams and no doubt the other missionary families when he laments the arrival of a ship direct from London with no letters on board.[93]

But in addition, the missionaries felt there was a bottleneck at Port Jackson. "The Registers which you send for the mission, had better be directed expressly for us," Williams wrote to London, "as they frequently find a corner in Mr Marsden's great house where they lay for many months."[94] Until the *Herald* was completed, regular supplies sent from Sydney were crucial for the survival of the mission, but Williams declared, "we have been driven almost to our wits end several times"[95] by delays, when numerous opportunities had seemed available. The result was that the missionaries had had to resort to sourcing supplies directly from local shipping at extortionate prices. Ordinarily the missionaries would have wished to have had as little dependence on the shipping as possible because of the negative influence that ships' crews had on the local Maori.

There were several other frustrations that Williams and the other missionaries experienced. Firstly, the placement of each of the

[93] H Williams to the Secretaries, 9 July 1824, *CMS Archives,* CNM3, 265; H Williams to the Secretaries, 30 September 1825, *CMS Archives,* CNM3, 532.
[94] H Williams to the Secretaries, 9 July 1824, *CMS Archives,* CNM3, 264.
[95] H Williams to the Secretaries, 31 March 1825, *CMS Archives,* CNM3 334.

missionaries was under Marsden's control. William Hall, whose health had deteriorated considerably, needed to be returned to the Colony, but no decision had been received from Marsden. Finally Hall presented his situation to the Local Committee of Missionaries and looked to them to give him the authority he needed to leave his station.[96]

There were either no decisions forthcoming from Marsden or there were ones that the missionaries considered inappropriate. For example, the Local Committee deemed it necessary, due to the difficult behaviour of the local Maori at Kerikeri, for Richard Davis to be moved to Paihia, but they knew it would be against Marsden's wishes.[97] Williams' response was that "Mr Marsden does not know these people: adhering to Mr Marsden's desires, both Mr Davis and the mission generally would have been involved in much difficulty."[98] In the end, Marsden's wishes were overturned by a Quarterly Meeting of missionaries, without his input.[99]

At other times, the Local Committee were frustrated by not being able to enforce their own majority decision. If differences of opinion arose, they could not be settled quickly and finally by the missionaries themselves. This perpetuated the disunity that had so afflicted the mission in the past and would work against Williams' plan to bring a greater level of cohesion to the mission team. A case in point was the state of the house at Kerikeri formerly occupied by Butler. In May of 1824, William Hall was asked by the Committee why he had not dismantled the vacant house as agreed upon at a previous meeting. The urgency of the matter was that valuable material needed to be reused elsewhere and had to be salvaged before it was all stolen. Hall's reply was that he hadn't done so because he was first wanting Marsden's opinion on the matter (presumably Hall

---

[96] Quarterly Meeting, 4 April 1825, *CMS Archives,* CNM4, 32.
[97] Due to his promise made to Hongi Hika and wanting to curb his warring by way of agriculture. Elder, *Letters and Journals,* 336-337, 383.
[98] H Williams to the Secretaries, 31 March 1825, *CMS Archives,* CNM3, 333.
[99] Quarterly Meeting, 10 July 1826, *CMS Archives,* CNM4, 213.

had disagreed with the original decision). The Committee decided that the matter could not wait for Marsden's view to be made known.[100]

---

[100] Monthly Meeting, 4 May 1824, *CMS Archives*, CN04/1. In the end it seems that the house remained standing and was then occupied by the newly arrived George Clarke and family.

8. Events Come to a Head

The issue of 'local control' became of increased strategic importance for Williams when his brother, William Williams, arrived in March 1826. Henry had lobbied long and hard to have his brother join him in New Zealand rather than being placed in India, the field where often the more academically able of the CMS missionaries were sent.[101] Henry Williams realised that if language learning and itinerant preaching were to take on a more prominent role within the Missions, then each of the stations would need a greater concentration of missionary personnel. Consequently, he very much wanted his brother and family to settle with him at Paihia. Marsden, for his part, was contemplating establishing a hospital on Moturoa Island and thought that William Williams (who trained as a surgeon) would be the ideal person to be placed there.[102]

These differences took on a new urgency at the beginning of May 1826, when Henry Williams received a letter from Richard Hill, informing him that a Corresponding Committee had just been formed in New South Wales under authorisation from the CMS in London and that this Committee, of which Hill was Secretary, would in future be "directing" the work of the New Zealand Mission.[103] Receiving this correspondence from Hill, provoked Williams into immediately writing a letter to the Parent Committee in London, in which he submitted a detailed critique of Marsden's mission strategy

---

[101] Henry Williams to the Secretaries, 21 November 1823 & 9 July 1824, *CMS Archives*, CNM3, 87 & 264.

[102] Marsden to the Secretaries, 2 February 1826, *CMS Archives*, CNM4, 79. *Missionary Register*, 1827, 123. See also Elder, *Letters and Journals*, 403.

[103] R Hill to H Williams, 10 May 1826, *CMS Archives*, CNM4, 170. See also *Missionary Register*, 1827, 120.

and requested a reform in the way the mission was governed.[104]

Before looking at this letter in more detail, it is interesting to note that by this time, letters usually took between five and six months to arrive in England. For instance, the letter that Henry Williams wrote eight months prior recounting the death-bed baptism of Christian Rangi, had arrived at CMS house within 5 months and was published in the *Missionary Register* in seven.[105] However, in 1826 all the letters addressed from New Zealand to England were not sent until the end of the year and arrived together in early May 1827.[106] This meant that the letter that Henry Williams wrote in May 1826 was not received in London until May 1827! In fact, it was received after the later letters that had passed between Williams, Marsden and Hill, in which Williams queries the function of the new Corresponding Committee in Sydney. The implication to be drawn is that the letters were sent as public letters via New South Wales and were held back by the newly formed Corresponding Committee. In this manner, the Corresponding Committee ensured that information was passed on to the Parent Committee in an orderly fashion. It was not that Sydney withheld information, for it did include a later letter from William Williams that outlined the same policy changes but written in a more diplomatic style and without the overt criticism of the strategy used by Marsden in the running of the mission.[107]

The reason for the delicate manoeuvring between New Zealand and Sydney was because it involved issues of authority and

---

[104] H Williams to D Coates, 15 May 1827, *CMS Archives*, CNO93/10 (copy CNM4, 171-176). There are six days (inclusive) between the dates of the respective letters, which is enough time for the voyage from Sydney to the Bay of Islands. H Williams' reply in July to Hill was to hand within five days of writing (*CMS Archives*, CNM4, 164-165).

[105] H Williams to the Secretaries, 30 September 1825, *CMS Archives*, CNM3, 531-540; *Missionary Register*, 1826, 185-188.

[106] Each letter is dated as it arrived in London. *CMS Archives*, CNM4, 171, 176, 179, 185, 204.

[107] W Williams to Marsden, 7 July 1826, *CMS Archives*, CNM4, 163-164.

the chain of command. As a military man, Henry Williams regarded obedience to orders as one of his highest duties. He was also well aware, before coming to New Zealand, of the problems caused by those who disregarded authorised instructions and had himself declared to the CMS Committee,

> "In the observances of the orders and wishes which you may from time to time send to me I shall ever consider it, I do assure you, as a most sacred duty to regard them as rigidly as ever I did those of my senior officer while I was in His Majesty's Service."[108]

It was therefore not an option for Henry Williams to simply seize control by default. In addition, his new strategy relied upon establishing a consensus amongst the missionaries themselves as to the new objectives that the mission should be pursuing. Williams needed the approbation of the Parent Committee in London, or at least the acquiescence of Parramatta.

Despite appearances, Williams would not have been too concerned about the delay in the delivery of his letter, as it was highly likely that the dispatch was sent as a public, not private letter. The implication being that the letter was forwarded to England via New South Wales with Williams' full intention that Marsden should also read it. In any case, London did not reply directly to Williams' letter until the December and so any reply would have reached New Zealand in May 1828 at the earliest, which was two years after Williams first put pen to paper.

---

[108] Rogers, *Te Wiremu*, 42.

9. William's Critique of Marsden's Strategy

The preceding discussion helps to highlight the significance of Henry Williams' letter to London (dated 15 May 1826), and marks that year as a significant turning point in the way in which the mission was conducted.[109] In the letter Williams stated his rather frank evaluation of Marsden's strategy and went on to give his rationale for the changes he and the Local Committee were intending to make. Williams was conscious of the fact that he was speaking out of turn, but felt that he had a higher responsibility to the "Christian world" which demanded that he speak freely.

Williams' key concern was that the missionaries were having all their time consumed by "temporal matters" to the point where the "spiritual" objectives of the mission were being neglected. He then asked the question, what was the root of this problem? Were the missionaries themselves to blame? Had they failed to carry out their duties as directed? This had been Marsden's previous conclusion when addressing the failings of the mission to date. However, Williams did not accept that conclusion and instead identified as the root cause, Marsden's policy of stressing the need to civilise Maori as a first step to receiving the Gospel. While Williams acknowledged that Marsden had done nothing other than what he had thought best for the mission and that he was still greatly respected by the missionaries, "but, still, with all his excellencies, we as a body, cannot but differ from him in opinion, as to the local management of affairs."

It was not that Williams wanted to simply rule out the benefit

---

[109] H Williams to Coates, 15 May, 1826, *CMS Archives*, CNO93/10 (or CNM4, 171-176; though note that the copyist has recorded the incorrect year of 1827 instead of 1826 as on the original). Unless otherwise stated, all references in this section are to this letter. See the appendix for a transcript of the letter.

of teaching Maori the "civil arts", but in his view, to pursue such an objective independently of also seeking a "renewed nature" was having detrimental outcomes for both the mission and Maori. He gave as an example the practise of paying Maori with trade goods to grow wheat. Maori generally did not wish to eat the wheat when grown, and having plenty of their own food, the surplus gave them the opportunity to trade it with the shipping for muskets and powder. To add insult to injury, because the missionaries had done so much to enable the cultivation to occur, it made them indirectly responsible for sustaining the very trade they detested!

Williams made mention of two other by-products from this fixation on agriculture. Firstly, that Maori were confused as to the motives of the missionaries and thought that they could only have been motivated by self-interest. Secondly, because the food was grown in only one local area, the market was swamped with trade items from the missionaries to the point where it became increasingly difficult to obtain Maori labour to assist in the work. Williams finished his critique by pointing out that they were frequently asked by Maori if they could receive instruction in reading and writing or if they could be visited on the Sabbath, "but I do not know one instance of their asking for instruction in temporal matters."

Thus Williams asked that the mission be allowed to be "newly modelled" with a "reform in the government of the Mission"; not simply a fresh approach, but that responsibility be devolved to those with first-hand experience. "Who," said Williams, "are most capable of giving an opinion ... we who are on the spot and have now had experience – or an individual or individuals, who are in the Colony of New South Wales, and have had no experience?" Here Williams revealed his fear that authority was in danger of passing, not from Marsden to the Local Committee, but to the newly formed Corresponding Committee, which would result in an even greater degree of uninformed decision making. In posing the question,

Williams does not discount the knowledge that Marsden had gained from his four subsequent visits to New Zealand (the third of which lasted over nine months[110]), but by the very nature of the visits, it had given him a misleading impression.

> "It is very obvious to us, that Mr Marsden, from the observations he had made from time to time, knows but little of the character of the New Zealander. Mr Marsden, in travelling, seldom saw the same people twice, and never continued long in one place; but dispensing his presents on every side, he had always numbers at command, yet learned but little of the real state of things."[111]

Williams asked why the strategy adopted for the New Zealand Mission should be so different to that of Africa or India. The instructions given for the running of the mission were not, in practice, creating the desired outcome, nor were they meeting the stated expectations of the Society. These included the particular instructions given to Williams when he departed from England, which he then goes on to quote at length, not for the benefit of the CMS Committee in London, of course, but so that Marsden might read them again more closely. The CMS in London had instructed Williams in the following terms:

> "It is the great and ultimate purpose of this Mission to bring the noble but benighted, race of New Zealanders, into the enjoyment of the light of the Gospel. To this grand end all the Society's measures are subordinate. This end, therefore, the Committee urge on you; and on every other Labourer in the Mission, to keep continually in view: and they are more earnest with you on this point, because, in the constant attention which this Mission will require for years to come to secular business, the temptation of the Labourers has been and will be, not to give a due proportion in their plans to

---

[110] Elder, *Letters and Journals*, 237.
[111] H Williams to Coates, *CMS Archives*, CN/O93/10 (or CNM4 207-209)

Religious Education and Instruction."[112]

"Your wishes here appear evident," said Williams, and the reason they had not been carried out was because of conflicting instructions from "Port Jackson". Here Williams wished to raise a further difference in strategy between himself and Marsden, which concerned the division of labour between clerical and lay missionaries. While it might be expected that the clerical members of the mission would be allowed to get on with the spiritual work at hand, Williams was concerned that the lay members had been specifically encouraged to concentrate on "temporal exertions." Yet as Williams reads his instructions from London, he noted that the same priorities were actually urged upon both groups.

Williams wanted the situation to be clarified for the sake of the lay settlers, for there was a "considerable misunderstanding upon this question". "Division in sentiment" was bad enough, but next to it was the evil of "division in occupation". What Williams wished to achieve was the harnessing of all the resources of the mission behind one common end, the conversion of the Maori. Which meant for Williams that they all had a share in the same work. The problem with the present strategy in his view, was that it made rivalry and competition between missionaries almost impossible to avoid, resulting in dissension and ill-feeling. But now there was a golden opportunity to make real changes, for it had been mutually agreed by the Local Committee that the present strategy was not working. "We are now of one view; and it is our opinion, that this people will be neither civilized nor Christianized, by our past mode of proceeding."

---

[112] Ibid.

10.   New Emphasis Proposed

It is at this point that Williams goes on to outline the changes that they wished to make. There were three areas, and each of them depend for their outcome on two new policies; firstly the policy of combining capacity of both the lay and clerical members behind the same common objectives and secondly, the placing of missionaries together in larger settlements rather than setting up new stations or spreading personnel out over a wide region.

The first area and arguably the most strategic of the three, was that of language learning. The missionaries had learnt enough of the Maori language for day to day purposes and for trade, but it was totally inadequate for interacting at a deeper apologetic level concerning the Gospel or for the work of Bible translation. Williams recognised that they must grapple with the grammar of the language if they were to begin serious translation work. And that could only be achieved if they came together and gave the task "intense application for a considerable time."

The second area involved an increased level of engagement with Maori over a wider geographical area through itinerant visitation. If the first priority of language study cloistered the missionaries away, the second counter-balanced that with an extension of their influence to a wider circle of Maori settlements. The new strategy would have the missionaries supplement their regular Sabbath day visiting to include more extended trips during the week. As this was best done in pairs, and bearing in mind the need for at least two Europeans to remain at each station at all times, it again required that the missionaries needed to live together in larger settlements and for the lay members to be full partners with the clergy in the work. As a consequence of their new duties, the only way that the lay members could be made available was if they were also relieved of a good portion of their "temporal" tasks, such as farming.

The third area that Williams outlined in his letter was the wish for a renewed focus on Maori education with both male and female schools. Here the strategy was less well developed apart from adapting established models already in use in England – that was "as far as our ideas of it extend," said Williams. But it did lead him to express his serious concern about the condition of Maori females, particularly because of their use as ship prostitutes: "They are not only viewed as far inferior to the Males, but at an early age are taken to the shipping from all parts of the Island at peace with these tribes." Consequently, female schools were especially important, but that would necessitate placing a larger burden on the missionary wives in addition to their own young families. This became another reason why, according to Williams, it was necessary for the mission to be "uniting our strength."

Williams finished the letter by drawing attention to the particular situation of Richard Davis, a lay missionary farmer whose original instructions from the CMS in London specified that he was to grow wheat for the mission. As previously mentioned, Davies had to be moved from Kerikeri to Paihia, even though it was contrary to Marsden's wishes. Williams, in an earlier letter, had spoken of how "the disposal of Mr Davis has occupied considerable time and consideration."[113] If the new policy was to be adopted, then its immediate impact would fall on Davis, who had been sent out with such a specific task, but currently found himself based at Paihia and sharing in the work of the other missionaries.[114] Williams considered it to be neither "desirable" or "practicable" to stick with his instructions as originally given. The work would suffer from all the attendant problems already mentioned in the letter and the total cost would make it twice that of simply shipping the wheat direct from New South Wales. Therefore, said Williams in closing his letter, they requested that Davies' previous instructions be recalled and that he be released to join the other missionaries in language learning and

[113] H Williams to the Secretaries, 31 March 1825, *CMS Archives*, CNM3, 333.
[114] Quarterly Meeting, 3 April 1826, *CMS Archives*, CNM4, 208.

"intercourse with the Natives – that he thereby may be enabled to declare unto them, the glad tidings of the Gospel of Peace." The wheat farmer had now become a lay catechist.

11.   Williams' Strategy Implemented

Williams wrote in a letter to the CMS in London, dated 16 October 1826, that from the arrival of William Williams in New Zealand, "we commenced upon our new system; which no doubt will continue."[115] There was good reason for Williams to continue, since there was now a growing sense of purpose and cohesion amongst the missionary band. In general, there seemed to be a consensus as to the new way forward. At the Quarterly Meeting of missionaries, July 1826, Kemp, Clarke and Hamlin all seemed to be relishing their new freedom. Even Davis conceded that trying to grow wheat at Kawakawa was indeed impractical and that his presence was needed at Paihia.[116] However, the real surprise and the one who embraced the new policies with the most vigour was James Shepherd.

Shepherd had only recently returned to the mission after a year of recuperation in the Colony. His time away was due to experiencing trouble with his eyes and other problems, including probably exhaustion.[117] But he was back with renewed energy and both Henry and William Williams remarked on the change. "Whatever may have been the failings of the latter [Shepherd] during his former residence on the Island," wrote William to Marsden, "he is now desirous to act very differently."[118] Henry reported, "We consider the shaking up he got at Mr Hall's has done him much service."[119] In particular, Shepherd was now demonstrating a real flair for the Maori language, and in Marsden's opinion had the better understanding of any of the others.[120] Shepherd reported to the July meeting that he had

---

[115] H Williams to the Secretaries, 16 October 1826, *CMS Archives*, CNM4, 176.
[116] Quarterly Meeting, 10 July 1826, *CMS Archives*, CNM4, 213.
[117] *Missionary Register*, 1825, 102; 1826, 157 & 161.
[118] W Williams to Marsden, 7 July 1826, *CMS Archives*, CNM4 210-214.
[119] H Williams to Marsden, 4 July 1826, *CMS Archives*, CNM4 161-163.
[120] Marsden to the Secretary, 25 April 1826, in Elder, *Letters and Journals*, 445.

commenced a translation of Matthew's Gospel and had collected phrases and arranged the vowels "according to their different terminations."[121]

The aptitude that Shepherd demonstrated, despite his background as a horticulturist, was indicative of the new calibre of missionary that would be required for the work. And William Williams was anxious to make that point clear to London when he wrote,

> "I wish to guard you against an opinion current in England, that any person is fit for New Zealand while those who have received more advantages in education should be sent to the more polished nations of the East. The mind of the New Zealander is if I mistake not by no means inferior to that of a Hindoo, and the language perhaps equally as copious... besides which the duty of a translator will always require at least a knowledge of the originals."[122]

There were still some tensions amongst them over placements and the maintenance of stations, particularly in regard to the oldest, Rangihoua. The wooden chimneys needed to be replaced for safety reasons, but was it better for the station to be re-located to the other side of the Maori *pá* (fortified village), to Te Puna, or closed altogether?[123] Closing Rangihoua might have allowed for the greater concentration of personnel that Williams was looking for and would have recognised the shift in population demographics around The Bay due to the current fighting, but the issue wasn't pushed. After so many years of difficult committee meetings, Williams was able to write in his journal at the end of 1826, "Our meetings upon all occasions are now very agreeable and refreshing. I trust by past experience, we are enabled to appreciate our present blessing in this

---

[121] Quarterly Meeting, 10 July 1826, *CMS Archives*, CNM4, 213.

[122] W Williams to the Assistant Secretary, 26 October 1826, *CMS Archives*, CNM4, 185-188.

[123] Quarterly Meeting, 10 July 1826, *CMS Archives*, CNM4 213; Monthly Meeting, 6 September 1826, *CMS Archives*, CNM4 457.

respect."[124]

As soon as the *Herald* returned from its maiden voyage to Port Jackson on 31 May 1826, plans were made for a trip to Tauranga to obtain the vital food supplies that were now required for the mission. It set off on 20 June and returned 3 July, laden with food "as deep as she would swim."[125] The trip to Tauranga was followed by two to the Hokianga (the first trip was aborted after it was judged too risky to cross the bar and enter the harbour, due to inexperience).[126]

By the end of 1826, the new emphasis on language learning was an integral part of the daily routine for the mission. The missionaries made it a priority to study together each morning so that no 'temporal' concerns would interrupt. Williams reported to the Quarterly Meeting in July that the missionaries at Paihia had set aside 9 o'clock to 12 noon for language study.[127] Kerikeri members reported to the October meeting that they too were now following a similar pattern.[128] Shepherd had made a start on the translation of Matthew's Gospel and William Williams was close behind, announcing to the October meeting that he had made a start on Genesis.[129] Others were showing a flair for the language as well, including William Puckey, the 21 year old son of a former LMS missionary, working at Paihia as a carpenter.[130] By the middle of 1827, the mission was ready to send R Davis to Sydney to oversee the printing of 400 copies of Scripture portions translated into Maori.[131] These 31 page booklets represented

[124] *CMS Archives,* CNM4, 233-243.
[125] H Williams to the Secretaries, 16 October 1826, *CMS Archive,* CNM4, 176.
[126] Ibid., 178.
[127] Quarterly Meeting, 10 July 1826, *CMS Archives,* CNM4 210-214.
[128] Quarterly Meeting, 10 October 1826, *CMS Archives,* CNM4 458.
[129] Quarterly Meeting, 10 October 1826, *CMS Archives,* CNM4 458.
[130] W Williams to Coates, 21 May 1827, *CMS Archives,* CNM4 358.
[131] Elder, *Letters and Journals,* 445; Rogers, *Te Wiremu,* 50; Peter J. Lineham, *Bible & Society: A Sesquicentennial Hisotry of the Bible Society in New Zealand* (Wellington: The Bible Society in New Zealand, 1996), 10. The 31 page booklet contained Genesis 1-3, John 1, Exodus 20. Matthew 6:1-30, the Lord's Prayer and seven hymns.

the tangible fruits of a new strategy that required many hours of intensive study. It also gave the missionaries a greater facility in speaking Maori, which was so important for their work in the schools and itinerant visiting.

The second part of Williams' strategy was a renewed emphasis on education for Maori. The running of schools had proved difficult for the missionaries, particularly since the departure of Kendall. Despite Marsden's encouragement to make greater efforts, there were other demands on the missionaries' time that had to take precedence.[132] Now that there was a better supply of food and a greater proficiency with the language, Williams was keen that each station should open a school for Maori who were in residence, both adults and children. They were given accommodation and food and in return, they attended daily worship with the missionaries, studied literacy and numeracy in the morning, while the afternoons were given over to the "acquisition of the civil arts,"[133] The students often included the sons and daughters of the local chiefs, or slaves given to or redeemed by the missionaries. Both of these groups proved to be highly strategic in the years ahead. Education was in Maori, because the aim was for students to read the Bible in Maori, an objective consonant with the overall strategy of communicating the Gospel message. Marsden was also supportive of providing schools, but in view of the connection with New South Wales, he felt that Maori needed to learn English.[134]   This would have fitted well with Marsden's policy of encouraging trade and commerce throughout Australasia.

The number of children reported as being under instruction rose from single figures in 1824, to 50-60 during the first part of 1826, but then doubled to over 120 from July onwards. Most of this increase was due to the opening of girls' schools at each of the

---

[132] *Missionary Register*, 1825, 102.
[133] H Williams to Coates, 15 May 1826, *CMS Archives*, CNM4, 171-176.
[134] *CMS Archives*, CNM4, 57.

stations.[135] Such an increase in numbers was only sustainable because of the sourcing of provisions from beyond The Bay by the *Herald*. It also, no doubt, increased the workload carried by the missionary wives.

Mission historian Cathy Ross writes about the role of missionary wives and their general invisibility in the archival records of the mission.[136] The reality was that "in fact immense amounts of work in schools and training was done by wives, un-listed daughters as well as companions and governesses."[137] The bustling nature of the missionary house, with its complete lack of privacy and the constant interaction with Maori through hospitality, work and education, belies the common perception of the missionary households as "tiny fragments of England sheltering behind a ring of picket fences and rambler roses."[138]

Although often unrecognised, the missionary family as an example of domestic Christian virtue was an intentional strategy adopted generally by missionaries of this period. Dana Robert comments, "despite its ubiquity in missionary thinking, this most enduring and successful aspect of mission theory has been forgotten in the scholarly discussion of Anglo-American mission thought."[139] The Christian family provided both an 'object lesson' for the unconverted and set an example of pious living for those being

---

[135] Figures sourced from the *Missionary Register*, 1825, 102, and the Quarterly Meetings of 2 January, 3 April, 10 July, 10 October 1826, *CMS Archives*, CNM4, 204-214 & 457-460.

[136] Cathy Ross, *Women with a Mission: Rediscovering Missionary Wives in Early New Zealand* (Auckland: Penguin Books, 2006), 12-13.

[137] Jocelyn Murray, "Anglican and Protestant Missionary Societies in Great Britain: Their Use of Women as Missionaries From the Late 18th Century to the Late 19th Century," *Exchange*, 21, 1, (April 1992), 7, quoted in Ross, *Women with a Mission*, 15.

[138] Judith Binney, introduction to *An Account of New Zealand and of the Church Missionary Society's Mission in the Northern Island, by William Yate* (Shannon: Irish University Press, 1970), v.

[139] Dana L. Robert, "The 'Christian Home' as a Cornerstone of Anglo-American Missionary Thought and practice," in Robert, *Converting Colonialism*, 135.

discipled. In providing education for Maori girls, it can not be assumed that the missionaries were simply introducing them "to middle-class English ways."[140] What is important in shaping this encounter, Robert argues, is the motivations and class assumptions of the missionaries in each particular context.[141] "Lower-middle-class missionaries," she writes, "whether British or American, may have seen domestic training as a key to self-reliance."[142] This is arguably the case in the Bay of Islands during the 1820s where female schooling was established with the express purpose of countering the use of Maori girls as ship prostitutes.[143]

In many ways, the schools fulfilled the same function for Williams as the seminary at Parramatta did for Marsden. The hope was that a number of their students would become a generation of indigenous evangelists to take the Gospel far beyond the reach of the mission station. By the year 1827, there were already reports of Maori closely associated with the mission moving to other districts, building churches and conducting services on the Sabbath.[144] The nurturing and training of indigenous evangelists was a natural consequence of the new emphasis on schooling.

The third component of Williams' new strategy was the regular visiting of Maori settlements within a 15 mile (24km) radius of the mission stations. This brought the missionaries into contact with a wider circle of Maori, and made them realise that their previous methods had been sending rather mixed messages. The assumption was, wrote George Clarke of Maori, that "we came among them with the design of serving ourselves: their land, their timber, their pigs, and their potatoes, they expected would most demand our attention."[145] This was something that Williams had

---

[140] Binney, *William Yate*, 7.
[141] Robert, *The 'Christian Home'*, 157.
[142] Ibid., 157.
[143] H Williams to Coates, 15 May 1826, *CMS Archives*, CNM4, 171-176.
[144] *Missionary Register*, 1828, 465.
[145] *Missionary Register*, 1826, 613.

pointed out in his letter of 15 May 1826: "it is generally thought by them that we come here on account of the goodness of their land, and to purchase their Pigs and Potatoes."[146]

Once it was recognised that the visits were not for the purpose of trade, a number of Maori soon lost interest.[147] Others were attracted to this new message that was brought, particularly to the historical sections of the Bible, although the missionaries found it harder to convince them of their need for salvation.[148] Williams wrote in 1824, "They believe that there is a great difference between our God and the God of the New Zealanders; but they content themselves with considering it very well for us to observe the orders of our God, and for themselves to remain under the jurisdiction of their own."[149]

A general outline of the type of message shared by the missionaries is given by Williams on the occasion of a visit to a village sometime in 1827:

> "The first words which [the chief] spoke were, "E parata" – a corruption of Brother, the name by which they always call me – 'I have forgotten the words which you told me to make use of in prayer, when you were at my place.' I then told him, that he must pray for the pardon of his sins, and for a new heart; and entered briefly into the particulars of our Lord's history, and His future coming to judge the world."

This dialogue featured such Christian concepts as "pardon of sins", a "new heart" and the future judgement. But it was conversations such as these that forced the missionaries to enter into the thought world of their hearers and re-clothe their message in concepts more familiar to a Maori worldview. For example, the Maori concept of *tapu* (something that is sacred or forbidden) was linked, via the Garden of

---

[146] H Williams to Coates, 15 May, 1826, *CMS Archives*, CNM4, 207-209.
[147] *Missionary Register*, 1826, 162.
[148] *Missionary Register*, 1826, 162.
[149] *Missionary Register*, 1826, 161.

Eden with the concept of sin.[150] Or, the concept of reciprocity (or *utu*), became an illustration of the atonement.[151] As the engagement became more developed, many other similar footholds for the Gospel were utilised which enabled a greater level of understanding on both sides of the exchange.[152]

What the missionaries were looking for in Maori, was for them to experience the 'great change' that came through receiving a new heart from God. As children of the evangelical awakenings of 18th century England, the missionaries were well used to this kind of language.[153] The concept of the heart also clearly resonated to some extent with Maori. Marsden had made this comment during his visit in 1823:

> "The New Zealanders are men of great reflection and observation; and they try to find out the motive for every thing which a man does. It is a very common observation with them, that 'the outside of a man may be seen, but the inside cannot,' and they frequently remark to me, after I have been conversing with any of their countrymen – 'You hear them speak, but you do not know what is in their hearts.' They study human nature with the closest attention, and endeavour to find out every man's real character from the whole of his conduct."[154]

Some Maori rejected the notion of a change of heart saying that they were satisfied with their native heart.[155] Others sought after that new heart of which the missionaries spoke. But, what did it mean for

---

[150] *CMS Archives*, CNM3, 260-261.

[151] *Missionary Register*, 1828, 463.

[152] For similar patterns of Christian interaction with primal societies see Harold Turner, "New Religious Movements in Primal Societies," 38-48.

[153] D. Bruce Hindmarsh, *The Evangelical Conversion Narrative: Spiritual Autobiography in Early Modern England* (Oxford: Oxford University Press, 2005), 333-336.

[154] *Missionary Register*, 1824, 513; Elder, *Letters and Journals*, 388.

[155] *Missionary Register*, 1830, 114.

Maori to experience a new heart? And how could the missionaries be sure that a work of God had truly taken place?

The level of detail given to the account of the baptism and death of Christian Rangi in September 1825, showed that the missionaries were pre-occupied by such questions.[156] They were also aware of the expectations of their supporters back in Britain for whom they wrote.[157] Christian Rangi's conversion was, for the missionaries, not only a celebration of one whose "soul was in heaven," but also as a 'proof of concept', that their native hearers were indeed able to receive the new birth according to the pattern they had expected.[158]

But as others wanted to respond to the Gospel message, things became less clear cut. For instance, Wini, Christian Rangi's brother, told Williams that he had responded to his message in the way required, but "Perhaps God will not hear us: we have called upon him for a long time, without perceiving any great change."[159] And Williams expressed in his journal his own uncertainty as to how to discern a person's true conviction: "They pray, moreover, according to our instruction, that the Spirit of God may be given to them to enlighten their hearts. More than this I cannot say; nor do I wish to be very sanguine, lest, after all, I should be deceived."[160]

---

[156] H Williams to the Secretaries, 10 September 1825, *CMS Archives*, CNM3, 531-540.
[157] *Missionary Register*, 1826, 185.
[158] Hindmarsh, *The Evangelical Conversion Narrative*, 329.
[159] *Missionary Register*, 1828, 463.
[160] *Missionary Register*, 1828, 464.

12. Marsden's Response

How did Marsden and the CMS in London respond to this new regime? It appears that London had already received advanced warning of the rumblings taking place in New Zealand and had somewhat pre-empted Williams.[161] Before receiving Williams' letter, they had written a letter (dated 30 September 1826) to clarify their view of the relationship between the primary objective of the mission and its subordinate means.[162] They declared the primary objective to be the "paramount duty" which they "urge upon every one... in the strongest manner" to "seek the spiritual good of the Natives... by the direct agency of the Gospel", but they "would not have you undervalue any subordinate means of attaining that end." They restated these views "because there appears to be a disposition in some of you, unduly to depreciate these subordinate means of advancing the objects of the mission." In describing the functioning of the "subordinate means" and their relationship to the Gospel, the language is in accord with Marsden's: they "tend to detach the Natives from the love of war," they encourage the "formation of habits of industry and order" and "under the blessing of God, very materially facilitate and enlarge the Missionaries opportunities of promoting the more direct objects of his mission." Neither would this letter have raised too many concerns for the New Zealand missionaries. For one thing, it did not finally arrive in The Bay until March the following year.

In the meantime, Marsden wrote a letter that Williams must have been nervously awaiting. It arrived on 17 October 1826 and

---

[161] The source of London's information has not been established but was most probably Marsden.

[162] Coates to the Brethren, 30 September 1826, *CMS Archives*, CNL1, 227-239. Unless otherwise stated, all further references in this section are from this letter.

showed that Marsden was not at all alarmed by the exchange of correspondence, in fact he was very pleased with the progress that was being made. He noted in his journal that Marsden "wrote with much satisfaction relative to the mission; and with much affection: expect him by the first Vessel."[163] Marsden finally arrived in New Zealand for a brief visit in April 1827 to settle on a plan for the education of the missionary children. There is no hint of any falling out between the two leaders, instead Marsden reported that "It gave me much pleasure to find the missionaries so comfortable, living in unity and godly love, devoting themselves to the work. I trust that the Great Head of the Church will bless their labours."[164]

Some years later, Marsden had an opportunity for a more lengthy visit to New Zealand in March 1830. Now aged 65, he recorded what might appear as a rather belated response to Williams' critique:

> "From the first formation of the Mission, I have always looked upon agriculture, as a secondary consideration, to hold out the best inducements for the Natives to form industrious habits; and, from that conviction, I have from time to time urged this important subject upon those employed in the Mission, not only for the general benefit of the Natives, but to guard themselves against the want of bread."[165]

This indicates that there was a continuing dialogue between Marsden and Williams over the role that agriculture was to play in pursuing the objects of the mission, this time in the context of establishing the new mission station at Waimate. This becomes clear when Marsden takes up the debate over a point previously made by Williams:

> "The argument which I have generally heard urged, by some individuals, against agriculture here, is, that flour could be prepared cheaper in New South-Wales than it could be in

---

[163] *Missionary Register*, CNM4, 181.
[164] Elder, *Letters and Journals*, 445.
[165] *Missionary Register*, 1831, 110.

New Zealand. Admitting this to be correct, which I cannot admit until experience has proved it to be so, it still appears to me most desirable that the Europeans should make the attempt to grow wheat. The Natives will never do it, unless the Europeans set them the example."[166]

It was not enough to tarnish the good-will that existed between both leaders. George Clarke recorded on the occasion of Marsden's visit:

"The good old gentleman's heart seemed to overflow with love and gratitude to God for what He had done; he said he could hardly have expected to see so much done in his day, knowing, as he did, the difficulties which were in the way of benefiting them in a spiritual point of view."[167]

---

[166] *Missionary Register*, 1831, 110-111.
[167] Elder, *Letters and Journals*, 495.

13. Conclusion

Examining in close detail the material gathered in this essay, we have been able to confirm two features concerning the mission strategies in New Zealand during the 1820s. Firstly, that 1826 was a significant turning point in the life of the New Zealand mission and secondly, that the reason for this change of direction was rooted in the differences between the strategic visions of Samuel Marsden and Henry Williams, and the passing of control from Parramatta to Paihia.

It was the beginning of 1826 that saw the launch of the mission ship, the *Herald*. This signalled the opportunity for Williams to finally implement the changes that until then had not been possible. Although it did allow the mission an increased level of independence from local Maori, this point can be pushed too far, for what was more significant was the increase in the level of food that could now be brought into the mission. The trip to Tauranga became more than simply an exercise in shopping, however, because it also marks arguably the first significant extension of the CMS mission to the South, beyond the Thames. Contact with Tauranga Maori was first established by the missionaries when they engaged a group of strangers in conversation while visiting the dying Christian Rangi at his settlement.[168]

1826 was also the year that saw the arrival of William Williams and the return of the rejuvenated James Shepherd. The significance of this lies in the greater level of commitment on behalf of the missionaries to come to grips with the Maori language as the cornerstone of their mission strategy for Bible translation, Maori education and itinerant preaching. Although all the missionaries

---

[168] This can be dated precisely from a letter of H. Williams as 24 July 1825. H. Williams to the Secretaries, 10 September 1825, *CMS Archives*, CNM3, 531-540.

participated in upgrading their language proficiency, it was the formation of Williams, Shepherd and Puckey into a translation team that particularly marks this year. The 'people movement' of Maori to Christianity during the 1830s and 40s would have been very different without having to hand the scriptures in Maori. The same can be said concerning the schools and their influence in the training of indigenous evangelists and the shaping of Christian Maori family and communal life.

This essay is entitled "To Plough or To Preach" and, of course, neither Samuel Marsden or Henry Williams would have been happy with such a simple dichotomy. For them, it was more a case of how each was to be prioritised, amidst the changing circumstances and contexts of the Mission. That is not so say, however, that there were not significant differences in how they conceived the mission in New Zealand and how it was to be implemented on the ground.

As we have seen, Marsden placed great emphasis on agriculture as a stimulus to industry and trade and a disincentive to pursuing the destructive power of war. He believed that the missionaries should be persistent in setting such an example for Maori to follow. In this, Marsden does appear to affirm a causal link between civilization and Christianity, but not as an impersonal 'rational' process in history or culture, but always as the action of God's grace in the life of God's people. This is the grand scheme that he envisaged for not only New Zealand, but the whole region of Australasia.

As a New Zealander, one can't help but feel that the popular Australian propensity to attribute avaricious motives to Marsden in his farming and trade interests is a failure on their part to glimpse something of the grandeur of his vision for the South Pacific. Marsden imbued his aspirations for Australia with all the romance of the Mayflower and the Pilgrim Fathers, including the irony of the circumstances, that God should use not "an army of pious Christians or men of character and of principle" but "men from the dregs of society – the sweepings of the gaols, hulks, and prisons."[169]

Williams, I think, could live with that, though he was probably still pressing the point over the establishment of the Waimate Station. Yet, we should not see Williams as rejecting evangelical humanitarianism in favour of a 'pure' preaching of God's word. It is just that it was manifested in different ways. It was shown in his concern for the Maori girls who were being abused for the sexual gratification of sailors, or his visiting of the sick and offering medical assistance. The missionaries themselves were unlikely, given their long-term resident status, to be the major vector for bring western diseases to the Maori. Though they did have to answer for the cruelty of their God in bringing diseases among them, and found themselves constantly having to challenge the Maori concept of *tapu* (forbidden, sacred); which as well as putting the patient into total isolation, deprived them of such basic care as food and water.[170]

The point that this essay has sought to make, is that although there were real differences between the strategies of Marsden and Williams, they should not be exaggerated. Both of them shared, along with the CMS in London, the same evangelical Calvinism that was commonplace amongst Anglican evangelicals of the day. This view refused a radical separation of 'Christianity' from 'civilization,' but neither did it view 'civilization' as the main object of the mission endeavour; instead it was simply an "accompaniment".[171] Dandeson Coates, the Lay Secretary of the CMS, in his official answer to Williams' letter of 15 May 1826 puts it nicely: "It hence appears," with regard to 'civilisation', "that the Missionary without making these specifically his object, becomes necessarily the Agent of producing them, if it please God to bless his labours to the spiritual good of the people."[172]

---

[169] *Missionary Register*, 1823, 66.
[170] *Missionary Register*, 1828, 464. Elder, 120-121.
[171] This view was articulated by the Scottish theologian Thomas Chalmers during the first part of the 19th century. See, Stanley, "Christianity and Civilization," 133.
[172] Coates to the Brethren, 19 June 1827, *CMS Archives*, CNLi, 265-267.

This is still a 'live' issue within world Evangelicalism, though the debate is now framed around the relationship between Evangelism and Social Responsibility.[173] The Lausanne Committee for World Evangelism after much discussion released a consultation report in which it described "at least three equally valid relationships" between Social Responsibility and Evangelism: 1. "Social action is a consequence of evangelism"; 2. "Social action can be a bridge to evangelism"; and 3. "Social action not only follows evangelism as its consequence and aim, and precedes it as its bridge, but also accompanies it as its partner." The report also affirms that "evangelism has a certain priority" because, at the end of the day, it "relates to people's eternal destiny." Both Marsden and Williams would have said, "Amen!"

As indicated in the introduction, there has been an antagonistic relationship between contemporary New Zealand historians and the early missionaries. For instance, Binney considers "the doctrine of civilisation, seen by the missionaries as a positive measure, was also fundamentally destructive."[174] In regard to the 'conversion,' Shroff writes, "The missionary technique of conversion was, in fact, to infect the Maori with a malady and then to offer Christ as a cure."[175] It is not the intention at this point to begin another, though very important, discussion; except to say that such readings of the missionary enterprise need to be carefully re-evaluated, as the archive records used in this essay can not support such conclusions.

What *is* revealed to us is the complex interaction of missionary and Maori, each products of their own social and religious culture, shaping one another by their encounter in ways that neither

---

[173] Material in this paragraph is quoted from Valdir R. Steuernagel, "Social concern and evangelization: The Journey of the Lausanne movement," *International Bulletin of Missionary Research* 15, no. 2 (April 1991): 53. Academic Search Complete, EBSCOhost (accessed October 27, 2009).

[174] Judith Binney, *The Legacy of Guilt: A Life of Thomas Kendall*, (1st edtion 1968) (Wellington: Bridget Williams Books, 2005) 38.

[175] G. W. Shroff, *George Clarke and the New Zealand Mission, 1824-1850* (master's thesis, Auckland University, 1967), 51, quoted in McLean, *No Continuing City*, 17.

could have predicted. The trouble with Binney's and Shroff's comments are that they are too one dimensional and static to be any longer helpful. Similarly, McLean's comment that "Nowhere was Marsden's 'simple-mindedness' more obvious than in his grasp of the importance of secular impacts on the spread of religious beliefs."[176] I hope that this essay has demonstrated that Marsden's approach to the mission enterprise in New Zealand was anything but simple, and involved the marshalling and stewarding of a complex array of resources to ensure an holistic approach to mission.

Stanley is more helpful when he reflects that, "the missionary project could not escape a commitment to assimilationism and the fundamental unity of humanity," but that such a commitment, "enabled evangelicals to articulate their sense of essential identity with, and urgent moral responsibility towards, the African people who were the victims of the slave trade."[177] We have seen a similar commitment from Marsden and Williams in the sources cited in this essay. Stanley goes on to say,

> "At least in the early nineteenth century, the evangelical emphasis ... was not on the inevitability of human progress towards the ideal of civilization, but rather on the capacity of universal human depravity to drag even the most ostensibly enlightened societies down the scale of degeneracy towards moral barbarism. It is this central feature of evangelical anthropology that prevented missionaries from giving a blank check to the forces of civilization."[178]

That the New Zealand missionaries adopted such an approach is demonstration by the way Williams confronted the Ships' Captains over their supply of guns to Maori.

---

[176] McLean, *No Continuing City*, 19.
[177] Stanley, "Christianity and Civilization," 172.
[178] Ibid., 173. Similar comments could be made re 'conversion', see D. Bruce Hindmarsh, "Patterns of Conversion in Early Evangelical History and Overseas Mission Experience," in Stanley, *Christian Missions and the Enlightenment*, 71-98.

"I tell the Captains they certainly will stand charged with murder, amongst other charges, in the great Day of Accounts: some say, they should gladly abstain from it; but were they [to abstain], while others continue, they should not obtain Supplies."[179]

In addition, Williams as a naval man himself, can not be considered merely prudish over his moral concerns regarding the shipping and the practise, "amongst other charges," of child prostitution in The Bay.

One of the reasons for writing this essay is to reclaim something of the heroic character of these narratives. They are not to be read as hagiography, but neither should they be dismissed as irrelevant to contemporary New Zealand society.[180] One of the reasons for dealing with this topic in such detail, is to avoid the problem of viewing history as merely an uncovering of the forces and processes that shape human society over time. The result of such an approach is that the 'actors' in the historical drama are reduced down to their supposedly essential 'character'. For example, Wright pays Marsden a back-handed compliment when he sums up his character as:

"a short, heavy, imposing, humorless man, and, as one might expect, not a very amiable one. Vindictive, contradictory, stubborn, vain, often intolerant – he was all of these; and yet there was something so magnificent about him that one cannot possibly dislike him."[181]

Such an impression can not be gained by reading the historical material identified in this essay. Nor is it all that important that we

---

[179] H. Williams to the Secretaries, 18 October 1826, *CMS Archives*, CNM4, 177.

[180] John Stenhouse, "God's own silence: secular nationalism, Christianity and the writing of New Zealand history," *New Zealand Journal of History* 38, no. 1 (2004): 52-71. With that in mind, it is disappointing that *The New Oxford History of New Zealand* does not contain a new study on the work of the missionaries. Giselle Byrnes, ed., *The New Oxford History of New Zealand*, ed. Giselle Byrnes (Melbourne: Oxford University Press, 2009).

[181] Wright, *New Zealand*, 39.

'like' Marsden. What these narratives help us to do, however, is to situate ourselves as contemporary New Zealanders in a real historical context rather than in some idealised secular Nirvana. It allows us to take seriously the way that we are shaped by events and ideas of the past and how our own actions today affect future generations.

14. Appendix

Rev Henry Williams to Dandeson Coates, Esq.

Marsden's Vale [Paihia], Bay of Islands

New Zealand, May 15, 1826

My Dear Sir,

Since my return from the Colony we have had much conversation amongst ourselves relative to the present state of the Mission, upon which, as standing peculiarly responsible to the Christian world, we consider it our duty to speak freely to you.

From the foundation of affairs here, little has yet been done towards the spiritual instruction of this people, owing to the general occupation in temporal matters and tho' from the circumstance of the case, as a body, we shall yet be required for a length of time to have our attention called aside occasionally; still we cannot but lament the general tenor of individual instruction, which appears to bear particularly upon the civilisation of this people, while preaching, studying, and translating, are not dwelt upon, and our force being scattered as it is, we are thereby exceedingly weakened.

To the present time Mr Marsden has disposed of the various members, and given such instruction as he considered to the interest of the Mission. This has now continued for a long period; and I think it may be said that since his last departure from the Island, his instructions have been observed as rigidly as possible. Our affection for Mr Marsden is very great, and though in the course of this letter we shall, of necessity, differ from him in opinion, we would wish to do it with perfect respect, and with the conviction that he has the interest of this people and of the Mission very near to him. But, still, with all his excellencies, we, as a body, cannot but differ from him in opinion, as to the local management of affairs.

May we not ask, who are most capable of giving an opinion, in reference to the station of the various Missionaries as they arrive, and to our general proceeding towards the Natives – we who are on the spot and have now had experience – or an individual or individuals, who are in the Colony of New South Wales, and who have had no experience? It may be said that Mr Marsden has had experience, and has travelled and spent many months here; but, then, it has been under such circumstances, as not to show the real character of the people. It is very obvious to us, that Mr Marsden, from the observations he has made from time to time, knows but little of the character of the New Zealander. Mr Marsden, in travelling, seldom saw the same people twice, and never continued long in one place; but dispensing his presents on every side, he had always numbers at command, yet learned but little of the real state of things.

Much stress has been laid upon the necessity of teaching the people the civil arts, husbandry, etc. This we grant is well in its place, though perhaps from the following remarks, it may be seen that the time is not yet arrived.

The Natives possess food and raiment in abundance; but from the use they apply them to, it evidently shows that they require a renewed nature: they need to be born again. It is but little of their produce that they either consume themselves, or bring to us, of that which is saleable; but it is reserved for the Shipping for Muskets and Powder; and though we do not supply them with these things, yet they are obtained through our means, by those articles of cultivation which are procured from us.

When the Natives are called to cultivate the land for wheat, or to saw timber they do not look beyond the present moment; and it has been generally thought by them that we come here on account of the goodness of their land, and to purchase their Pigs and Potatoes. But one very considerable evil attending the employing of many men, is, that of throwing a bulk of trade into one quarter, by which they become indifferent to work, and soon imbibe an avaricious and insolent disposition. For a long time past we have experienced great inconvenience, owing to the quantity of trade

64

possessed by the Natives in the neighbourhood. They have perpetually told us that they will not supply us with potatoes and corn (the food for the Natives in our employ and in the Schools) as they have plenty of Axes and Hoes, and in every thing else it is the same. The Natives will continue no longer at their work than one of us be with them to overlook, and also to partake in the labour: in short, there is not any thing to be done, but we are required to be in attendance, in addition to the perpetual hindrance from strangers coming about us, and the case of our respective families.

In all the efforts to civilize they do not perceive that we have any views beyond that of benefitting ourselves; and in some cases they have viewed with jealousy our purchasing of land.

Something of late has been done in behalf of Schools, sufficient to show how weak we are. The children ought to be under the eye of some one of us at all times, to direct their attention from mischief; but in reference to female Schools, this has been found impossible as yet, there being a young family in every house. The Natives around us have frequently asked us to give them instruction in reading and writing, and to visit them on the Sabbath and on other opportunities; but I do not know one instance of their asking for instruction in temporal matters.

May we ask why it is, that such a different mode should be adopted here to that pursued in other Missions – in Africa and India? We have no doubt as to the great end of your desires – to bring this people acquainted with their present state; and with that salvation which has been wrought for them. We are, therefore, at a loss to understand, why the majority of our small body should have instructions apparently of a different nature. If you compare the Report of this Mission with that of any other, you will perceive, that, while in the other fields the seed of the word of life has been scattered, here the main toil has been for the bread which satisfieth not: and this has been according to instructions. It may be said that cultivation is but part of the instruction, but still, when all the accompanying inconveniences are considered, it will be seen, that those who are so engaged, have much to contend with, and are subject to unnecessary mortification of mind; besides having their time destroyed for other duties. Still, individuals have not been left to a choice upon the question; as, had they not engaged in this, neither would they have eaten bread.

It has been our unanimous desire, that our specific duty be seriously considered by you – that the Mission be newly modelled, so as to enable the efforts of, not only a part, but of the whole body, to be brought into action.

In your various Letters you urge Schools, and private Letters evidently show the expectation of the Christian World; but the Mission has been groaning under temporal engagements, which have not tended to the benefit either of ourselves or the Natives. And in your Instructions to myself, you state that, "It is the great and ultimate purpose of this Mission to bring the noble but benighted, race of New Zealanders, into the enjoyment of the light of the Gospel. To this grand end all the Society's measures are subordinate. This end, therefore, the Committee urge on you; and on every other Labourer in the Mission, to keep continually in view: and they are the more earnest with you on this point, because, in the constant attention which this Mission will require for years to come to secular business, the temptation of the Labourers has been and will be, not to give a due proportion in their plans to Religious Education and Instruction."

Your wishes here appear evident; but why have they not been strictly adhered to? Is it from any evasion on the part of the Members of the Mission? – or have they attended to secular concerns, in addition to the erection of houses as according to their instructions from Port Jackson? Much has been said to Misters King, Hall, Kemp, R. and C. Davis, and Hamlin, to urge them to temporal exertions.

There has been, and evidently is, a considerable misunderstanding upon this question; and there perhaps, never has occurred, a more favourable opportunity, to enable such persons to know clearly what is expected from him, or, as a body, how we are to act. We are now of one view; and it is our opinion, that this people will be neither civilized nor Christianized, by our past mode of proceeding.

You have seen much mischief resulting from division of sentiment in this land. And the advantage Satan has gained at times. Surely, next to this, is the evil of division in occupation. Each having a different pursuit from the other, it is almost impossible but unhappy feelings will arise in the mind: each will wish to have his own department prosper, and will unintentionally appear to trespass.

For many months, there has been but one opinion. Permit us then to request a reform in the government of the Mission, that we may have but one pursuit – the making known to this people a Saviour's love.

Perhaps it may be well to state briefly our ideas relative to these questions.

Our communications with the Natives, can be only by one channel – that is the language. This, therefore appears to be the first point to be attained. But what a field does this open before us? To this the work of a day, a month, or a year? It will require intense application for a considerable time, and that not of one Individual but of the whole body. Each sentence must be examined strictly; and much writing is connected with it. It is a Language exceedingly copious, far beyond your idea of it.

The Natives ought to be visited, not merely on the Sabbath, but thorough the week, to the distance of fifteen miles around. There are four important places in connection with this Station (Marsden's Vale); i.e. Taiamai, a populous district, inland in a South West direction; where our people have cultivation: the Kawakawa, to the South East: and the inland Settlement of Tikoki [Tekoki], which has within these few months doubled its inhabitants, from various parts of the Bay: the Waikadi [Waikare], a large river which runs to the eastward with numerous Settlements on each side, and the Settlements toward the North West more immediately in the neighbourhood; each of these districts would require two Missionaries through the week, besides the attendance on the Schools. The Kedikedi [Kerikeri] has some small Settlements on each side of the river, but the Waimate, Pukenui, and Moubare [?]; at about 12 miles are important places. Rangihu [Rangihoua] is a considerable Settlement, and there are several others in a N. West direction – at Mataudi [Matauri], 15 miles distant, which is numerously inhabited.

It is not thought proper that we should travel singly; but go out two and two. More over that no more Stations ought to be formed for a considerable time, but the present ones reinforced; as from our past experiences we find it far more desirable that we should form a strong body where we now are, than be scattered more about. By residing in a number together, we are not so subject to the insolence of occasional visitors, as we are otherwise. The temporal duties of the Station may be superintended by one person for a given time; which will lighten these things considerably. Not less than two Europeans ought to be left in a Settlement, for any length of time; as no dependence can be placed upon these people.

In reference to the Boys' School, it is considered that they should be regulated according to the Military School at Chelsea, as far as our ideas of it extend:– that the former part of each day should be appropriated to reading, writing, and arithmetic; and the afternoon to the acquisition of the civil arts, according to the various dispositions; and that they should also generally make their own clothing. And that the Female Schools be modelled according to the Schools of Industry in various parts of England.

The condition of the females requires seriously to be considered. At present, the situation is very degraded. They are not only viewed as far inferior to the Males, but at an early age are taken to the shipping from all parts of the Island at peace with these tribes. As in every house in the Mission there is a young family, it will require a considerable effort, on the part of our Wives to attend to this duty; but we doubt not but that it may be effectually accomplished with care and by uniting our strength.

We feel it our duty to speak upon the occupation of Mr R Davis. It appears by your instructions to him that it is your wish that he should cultivate wheat for the Mission. Perhaps it may not be necessary to enter upon all the particulars of our ideas on this question; but we wish to state briefly first, that we do not think it desirable; and secondly, that we do not think it practicable.

In order to accomplish this expected cultivation, Mr Davis would be obliged to give up the whole of his time; for it would be necessary that he should be continually with the working people, and the quantity of trade which would have to pass through his hands to the tribe he might live with, would be more than they could endure, and would consequently be attended with a serious injury to their minds: they are young as yet, and may be compared to Children. Again, as they consider his object is for his own benefit and not for theirs, every thing that is to be done must be by extreme exertion. The expense of raising wheat here is far beyond the idea of any one who has not had experience. The wages and food of Natives, and the expenses of the European who superintends them, from seed time until it is turned into flower, are considerable; in many cases, doubling the price of the wheat which is sent from the Colony. The raising of a crop too is very precarious: any individual can with impunity set fire to it; or it may be set on fire by accident, as the country in the summer is frequently on fire for several miles in extent.

The impracticability of Mr Davis's furnishing wheat for the Mission appears to us evident, for want of means. The Natives will not work; that is, to that extent which it will be necessary to such an undertaking.

We therefore, considering the value of Mr Davis's services in the Mission, and how important it is that his zeal and talents should be directed to more serious objects, would earnestly request that your former Instructions to him, might be recalled; and that he should be permitted to labour in the acquisition of the Language and in intercourse with the Natives – that he thereby may be enabled to declare unto them, the glad tidings of the Gospel of Peace.

By request of the Committee,

(signed) Henry Williams.

BIBLIOGRAPHY

Bawden, Patricia. *The Years Before Waitangi: A Story of Early Maori/European Contact in New Zealand*. Auckland: Benton Ross, 1987.

Bennett, James. *Memoirs of the Life of Rev. David Bogue, D.D.* London, 1827.

Binney, Judith. "Christianity and the Maoris to 1840: A Comment." *New Zealand Journal of History* 3, no. 2 (1969): 143-165.

Binney, Judith. Introduction to *An Account of New Zealand and of the Church Missionary Society's Mission in the Northern Island*, by William Yate, i-vii. Shannon: Irish University Press, 1970.

Binney, Judith. *The Legacy of Guilt: A Life of Thomas Kendall*. Wellington: Bridget Williams Books, 2005. First published 1968 by Oxford University Press.

Byrnes, Giselle, ed. *The New Oxford History of New Zealand*. Melbourne: Oxford University Press, 2009.

Carleton, Hugh. *The Life of Henry Williams*. Auckland, 1874.

Church Missionary Society Archives. Special Collects. Birmingham University Library.

Clover, G. "'Going Mihinare', 'Experimental Religion', and Maori Embracing of Missionary Christianity - A Re-Assessment." *Christian Brethren Research Fellowship Journal* 121, no. 1 (1990): 41-55.

Davidson, Allan K., and Peter J. Lineham. *Transplanted Christianity: Documents illustrating aspects of New Zealand Church History*. 2nd edition. Palmerston North: Dunmore Press, 1989.

Elder, J. R. *The Letters and Journals of Samuel Marsden 1765-1838*. Dunedin: Wilkie & Reed for the Otago University Council, 1932.

Fisher, R. "Henry Williams' Leadership of the CMS Mission to New Zealand." *New Zealand Journal of History* 9 (1975): 142-153.

Gunson, Niel. *Messengers of Grace: Evangelical Missionaries in the South Seas, 1797-1860*. Melbourne: Oxford University Press, 1978.

Haweis, Thomas. *An Impartial and Succinct History of the Rise, Declension, and Revival of the Church of Christ*. Vol. 3. London, 1800.

Haweis, Thomas. The Blessings of Peace. London, 1801.

Hindmarsh, D. Bruce. "Patterns of Conversion in Early Evangelical History and Overseas Mission Experience." In Stanley, *Christian Missions and the Enlightenment*, 71-98.

Hindmarsh, D. Bruce. The Evangelical Conversion Narrative: Spiritual Autobiography in Early Modern England. Oxford: Oxford University Press, 2005.

Hiney, Tom. *On the Missionary Trail: A Journey Through Polynesia, Asia, and Africa with the London Missionary Society*. New York: Grove Press, 2000.

Howe, K.R. "The Maori Response to Christianity in the Thames-Waikato Area, 1833-1840." *New Zealand Journal of History* 7 (1973): 28-46.

Jenkins, Philip. *The Next Christendom: the Coming of Global Christianity*. New York: Oxford University Press, 2002.

Lineham, Peter J. *Bible & Society: A Sesquicentennial Hisotry of the Bible Society in New Zealand*. Wellington: The Bible Society in New Zealand, 1996.

Marsden, J. B. *Life and Work of Samuel Marsden*. Christchurch, 1913.

Maxwell, Ian Douglas. "Civilization or Christianity? The Scottish Debate on Mission Methods, 1750-1835." In Stanley, *Christian Missions and the Enlightenment*, 123-140.

McLean, Gavin. *No Continuing City: A History of the Stone Store, Kerkeri*. Wellington: New Zealand Historic Places Trust, 1994.

Missionary Register. London, 1820-1831.

Owen, J.M.R. "Christianity and the Maoris to 1840." *New Zealand Journal of History* 2, no. 1 (1968): 18-40.

Owens, J.M.R. "New Zealand before Annexation." In *The Oxford History of New Zealand: Second Edition*, edited by Geoffrey W. Rice, 28-53. Auckland: Oxford University Press, 1992.

Pickett, Waskom J. *Christian Mass Movements in India: a Study with Recommendations*. 2nd Indian Edition. Lucknow, India: Lucknow, 1969.

Piggin, Stuart. *Making Evangelical Missionaries 1789-1858: The Social Background, Motives and Training of British Prostestant Missionaries to India*. Courtenay Press, 1984.

Robert, Dana L., ed. *Converting Colonialism: Visions and Realities in Mission History, 1706-1914*. Cambridge: Eerdmans, 2008.

Robert, Dana L. Introduction to Robert, *Converting Colonialism*, 1-20.

Robert, Dana L. "The 'Christian Home' as a Cornerstone of Anglo-American Missionary Thought and practice." In Robert, *Converting Colonialism*, 134-165.

Rogers, Lawrence M. *Te Wiremu: A Biography of Henry Williams*. Christchurch: Pegasus, 1973.

Ross, Cathy. *Women with a Mission: Rediscovering Missionary Wives in Early New Zealand*. Auckland: Penguin Books, 2006.

Scotland, Nigel A.D. *Evangleical Anglicans in a Revoluntary Age: 1789-1901*. Carlisle: Paternoster, 2004.

Sinclair, Keith. *A History of New Zealand*. revised ed. Auckland: Penguin Books, 2000.

Skevington Wood, Arthur. *Thomas Haweis: 1734-1820*. London: SPCK, 1957.

Stanley, Brian. "Christianity and Civilization in English Evangelical Mission Thought, 1792-1857." In Stanley, *Christian Missions and the Enlightenment*, 169-197.

Stanley, Brian, ed. *Christian Missions and the Enlightenment*, edited by Brian Stanley, 169-197. Grand Rapids, MI: Eerdmans, 2001.

Stenhouse, John. "God's own silence: secular nationalism, Christianity and the writing of New Zealand history." *New Zealand Journal of History* 38, no. 1 (2004): 52-71.

Steuernagel, Valdir R. "Social concern and evangelization: The Journey of the Lausanne movement." *International Bulletin of Missionary Research* 15, no. 2 (April 1991): 53-56.

Tippett, Alan R. *People Movements in Southern Polynesia: Studies in the Dynamics of Church-planting and Growth in Tahiti, New Zealand, Tonga, and Samoa.* Chicago: Moody Press, 1971.

Turner, Harold. "New Religious Movements in Primal Societies." In *Australian Essays in World Religions*, edited by Victor C. Hayes, 38-48. Bedford Park, SA: The Australian Association for the Study of Religions, 1977.

Walls, Andrew F. "The Legacy of David Livingstone." *International Bulletin of Missionary Research* 11, no. 3 (July 1987): 125-129.

Walls, Andrew F. "The Legacy of Thomas Foxwell Buxton." *International Bulletin of Missionary Research* 15, no. 2 (April 1991): 74-78.

Wright, Harrison M. *New Zealand, 1769-1840: Early Years of Western Contact.* Cambridge, MA: Harvard University Press, 1959.

Yarwood, A.T. "Samuel Marsden." In *Australian Dictionary of Evangelical Biography*, edited by Brian Dickey, 250. Sydney: Evangelical History Assosciation, 1994.

Yarwood, A.T. *Samuel Marsden: The Great Survivor.* 2nd edition. Melbourne: Melbourne University Press, 1996.

LS 01   The Evangelical Anglican
         Identity Problem –
         Jim Packer

LS 02   The ASB Rite A Communion:
         A Way Forward –
         Roger Beckwith

LS 03   The Doctrine of Justification
         in the Church of England –
         Robin Leaver

LS 04   Justification Today: The
         Roman Catholic and Anglican
         Debate –
         R. G. England

LS 05/06 Homosexuals in the Christian
         Fellowship –
         David Atkinson

LS 07   Nationhood: A Christian
         Perspective – O. R. Johnston

LS 08   Evangelical Anglican Identity:
         Problems and Prospects –
         Tom Wright

LS 09   Confessing the Faith in the
         Church of England Today –
         Roger Beckwith

LS 10   A Kind of Noah's Ark? The
         Anglican Commitment to
         Comprehensiveness –
         Jim Packer

LS 11   Sickness and Healing in the
         Church –   Donald Allister

LS 12   Rome and Reformation
         Today: How Luther Speaks to
         the New Situation –
         James Atkinson

LS 13   Music as Preaching: Bach,
         Passions and Music in
         Worship –   Robin Leaver

LS 14   Jesus Through Other Eyes:
         Christology in a Multi-faith
         Context – Christopher Lamb

LS 15   Church and State Under God
         – James Atkinson

LS 16   Language and Liturgy –
         Gerald Bray, Steve
         Wilcockson, Robin Leaver

LS 17   Christianity and Judaism:
         New Understanding, New
         Relationship –
         James Atkinson

LS 18   Sacraments and Ministry in
         Ecumenical Perspective –
         Gerald Bray

LS 19   The Functions of a National
         Church –   Max Warren

LS 20/21 The Thirty–Nine Articles:
         Their Place and Use Today
         Jim Packer, Roger Beckwith

LS 22   How We Got Our Prayer
         Book – T. W. Drury,
         Roger Beckwith

LS 23/24 Creation or Evolution: a False
         Antithesis? –
         Mike Poole, Gordon Wenham

LS 25   Christianity and the Craft –
         Gerard Moate

LS 26   ARCIC II and Justification –
         Alister McGrath

LS 27   The Challenge of the
         Housechurches –
         Tony Higton, Gilbert Kirby

LS 28   Communion for Children?
         The Current Debate –
         A. A. Langdon

LS 29/30 Theological Politics –
         Nigel Biggar

LS 31   Eucharistic Consecration in
         the First Four Centuries and
         its Implications for Liturgical
         Reform –   Nigel Scotland

LS 32   A Christian Theological
         Language –   Gerald Bray

LS 33   Mission in Unity: The Bible
         and Missionary Structures –
         Duncan McMann

LS 34   Stewards of Creation:
         Environmentalism in the
         Light of Biblical Teaching –
         Lawrence Osborn

LS 35/36 Mission and Evangelism in
         Recent Thinking: 1974–1986
         –   Robert Bashford

LS 37 Future Patterns of Episcopacy: Reflections in Retirement – Stuart Blanch

LS 38 Christian Character: Jeremy Taylor and Christian Ethics Today – David Scott

LS 39 Islam: Towards a Christian Assessment – Hugh Goddard

LS 40 Liberal Catholicism: Charles Gore and the Question of Authority – G. F. Grimes

LS 41/42 The Christian Message in a Multi-faith Society – Colin Chapman

LS 43 The Way of Holiness 1: Principles – D. A. Ousley

LS 44/45 The Lambeth Articles – V. C. Miller

LS 46 The Way of Holiness 2: Issues – D. A. Ousley

LS 47 Building Multi–Racial Churches – John Root

LS 48 Episcopal Oversight: A Case for Reform – David Holloway

LS 49 Euthanasia: A Christian Evaluation – Henk Jochemsen

LS 50/51 The Rough Places Plain: AEA 1995

LS 52 A Critique of Spirituality – John Pearce

LS 53/54 The Toronto Blessing – Martyn Percy

LS 55 The Theology of Rowan Williams – Garry Williams

LS 56/57 Reforming Forwards? The Process of Reception and the Consecration of Woman as Bishops – Peter Toon

LS 58 The Oath of Canonical Obedience – Gerald Bray

LS 59 The Parish System: The Same Yesterday, Today And For Ever? – Mark Burkill

LS 60 'I Absolve You': Private Confession and the Church of England – Andrew Atherstone

LS 61 The Water and the Wine: A Contribution to the Debate on Children and Holy Communion – Roger Beckwith, Andrew Daunton–Fear

LS 62 Must God Punish Sin? – Ben Cooper

LS 63 Too Big For Words?: The Transcendence of God and Finite Human Speech – Mark D. Thompson

LS 64 A Step Too Far: An Evangelical Critique of Christian Mysticism – Marian Raikes

LS 65 The New Testament and Slavery: Approaches and Implications – Mark Meynell

LS 66 The Tragedy of 1662: The Ejection and Persecution of the Puritans – Lee Gatiss

LS 67 Heresy, Schism & Apostasy – Gerald Bray

LS 68 Paul in 3D: Preaching Paul as Pastor, Story–teller and Sage – Ben Cooper

LS69 Christianity and the Tolerance of Liberalism: J.Gresham Machen and the Presbyterian Controversy of 1922 – 1937 – Lee Gatiss

LS70 An Anglican Evangelical Identity Crisis: The Churchman – Anvil Affair of 1981–1984 – Andrew Atherstone

LS71 Empty and Evil: The worship of other faiths in 1 Corinthians 8-10 and today – Rohintan Mody

LATIMER PUBLICATIONS

LS72	To Plough or to Preach: Mission Strategies in New Zealand during the 1820s – Malcolm Falloon	
LS73	Plastic People: How Queer Theory is changing us – Peter Sanlon	
LB01	The Church of England: What it is, and what it stands for – R. T. Beckwith	
LB02	Praying with Understanding: Explanations of Words and Passages in the Book of Common Prayer – R. T. Beckwith	
LB03	The Failure of the Church of England? The Church, the Nation and the Anglican Communion – A. Pollard	
LB04	Towards a Heritage Renewed – H.R.M. Craig	
LB05	Christ's Gospel to the Nations: The Heart & Mind of Evangelicalism Past, Present & Future – Peter Jensen	
LB06	Passion for the Gospel: Hugh Latimer (1485–1555) Then and Now. A commemorative lecture to mark the 450th anniversary of his martyrdom in Oxford – A. McGrath	
LB07	Truth and Unity in Christian Fellowship – Michael Nazir-Ali	
GGC	God, Gays and the Church: Human Sexuality and Experience in Christian Thinking – eds. Lisa Nolland, Chris Sugden, Sarah Finch	
WTL	The Way, the Truth and the Life: Theological Resources for a Pilgrimage to a Global Anglican Future – eds. Vinay Samuel, Chris Sugden, Sarah Finch	
AEID	Anglican Evangelical Identity – Yesterday and Today – J.I.Packer and N.T.Wright	
IB	The Anglican Evangelical Doctrine of Infant Baptism – John Stott and J.Alec Motyer	
BF	Being Faithful: The Shape of Historic Anglicanism Today – Theological Resource Group of GAFCON	
FWC	The Faith we confess: An exposition of the 39 Articles – Gerald Bray	

Lightning Source UK Ltd.
Milton Keynes UK
30 January 2010

149323UK00002B/7/P